Railway World

ANNUAL 1988

£6.00

Nº 3

Railway World ANNUAL 1988

Edited by PETER JOHNSON

LONDON

IAN ALLAN LTD

Contents

First published 1987

ISBN 0 7110 1698 4

Published by Ian Allan Ltd, Shepperton, Surrey; and printed by Ian Allan Printing Ltd at their works at Coombelands in Runnymede, England

Cover:
Preserved Great Western Railway 'City' class 4-4-0 No 3440 *City of Truro* on the turntable at Scarborough on 20 December 1986. *Mike Spencer*

The Manning Wardle Pedigree

Mark Smithers

Of the many industrial locomotives which at present await the day when the necessary finance and labour resources can be found to enable them to operate once more, few can claim to be as historically important as *Sharpthorn*, the Manning Wardle saddle tank now residing at the Sheffield Park terminus of the Bluebell Railway. This is because she is the United Kingdom's oldest surviving product of the Boyne Engine Works of Leeds, and therefore the oldest home-based representative of a line of locomotive development which spanned the period from before the Crimean War to the middle of World War 2. Although the Manning Wardle standard designs were constructed for collieries and other industrial concerns throughout the firm's existence, it must also be remembered that many of their products were also supplied for the use of contractors engaged on the construction of a significant proportion of Britain's railway network. The London extension of the Manchester, Sheffield & Lincolnshire Railway, the Settle & Carlisle and the author's local Guildford-Cobham-Waterloo line were all built with the assistance of Manning Wardle locomotives. In addition to their employment by contractors and in industry, the firm's products played a major part in the locomotive history of the Colonel Stephens Railways, and in this context the best-remembered representatives are probably *Sidlesham, Morous* and *Ringing Rock* of the Hundred of Manhood and Selsey Tramways.

Any discussion of the origins of the Manning Wardle standard designs must naturally begin with events which took place at the Railway Foundry, Leeds, the premises of E. B. Wilson & Co, who were most famous for the 'Jenny Lind' design of 1846. However, before any detailed analysis of their development can be undertaken, certain points in relation to the standard Manning Wardle products should be noted. With the exception of the 18in gauge 'CHT' class, which was built in comparatively small

Left:
***Samuel Williams No 4* on display at Dagenham on 28 September 1968. This Manning is now on the Bluebell Railway, where it is known as *Sharpthorn*.** *H. S. Gamble*

numbers, there were essentially two basic types of design: the inside cylindered 0-6-0ST and the outside cylindered 0-4-0ST. The former were designated by the letter series 'I' (old) to 'Q', excluding 'P' and the latter by the series 'B' to 'I' and 'P'. In each case, the letter allocated to a particular class depended upon the locomotive's dimensions; the larger the locomotive the closer the class letter to the end of the alphabet. As well as the manufacturer's typical detail embellishments, the main similarities between the two basic specifications were that both were inside framed (the reason for excluding the 'CHT' class from consideration here) and that both utilised a design of boiler in which the conventional steam dome was replaced by a raised outer firebox casing which was used for steam collection purposes. As historical events turned out, it was this boiler design which was the earliest distinguishing mechanical feature of the Manning Wardle standard classes to evolve and it is this evolution that we must now turn to for consideration.

The basic principle of the use of a steam collecting space located over the firebox in conjunction with a boiler barrel devoid of mountings is firmly rooted in antiquity as far as locomotive genealogy is concerned. The 'Bury' type locomotive, of which the preserved ex-Furness Railway *Coppernob* is an example, is very much a representative of this school of thought, and here the outer part of the firebox is hemispherical in configuration. The various Stephenson long-boiler designs of the mid-1840s were applications of the same principle, but in this instance the famous 'Gothic' firebox prevailed. The precise date at which the plain inverted U-shaped raised firebox wrapper started to appear on boilers of this type is unclear, but in the context of Railway Foundry designs it is interesting to note that movement in this direction can be discerned as early as 1848. In that year David Joy (who was at that stage still in office as Chief Draughtsman for E. B. Wilson & Co) designed a freak 0-4-2 locomotive for the South Yorkshire Railway incorporating what was patented as the 'Cambrian' system of drive. Because of difficulties in obtaining the steam-tight working of this system, E. B. Wilson left the locomotive's construction to Thwaites Bros of Bradford, but the drawing of the locomotive which appears in E. L. Ahrons' *The British Steam Locomotive 1825-1925* and other publications shows a boiler with a plain raised firebox wrapper surmounted by a moderate size dome. By 1850, the year in which David Joy left the Railway Foundry for the first time, a class of dummy-crankshaft Crampton locomotives had been designed, with representatives going to the York & North Midland, the Ambergate, Nottingham, Boston & Eastern Junction, and (probably in the form of a larger design) the Kendall & Windermere lines. Of the several illustrations which survive of these locomotives, perhaps the most interesting is the contemporary engraving which appears in Mike Sharman's *The Crampton Locomotive*, which shows that by this stage the dome had disappeared altogether, but on some engines at least, a manhole cover surrounding the safety valve casing (but of considerably greater diameter) could still be seen to protrude through the firebox cladding. The Manning Wardle boiler had in all its essentials arrived on the scene, therefore, and two years later it was very much in evidence on a design of broad-gauge 0-4-0 well tanks. Although somewhat exaggerated claims have been made as regards the quantity of these locomotives which were produced, there have apparently been a mere two examples positively identified. No 329 of 1852 was of course the famous *Queen* of the Torbay & Brixham Railway, whilst No 454 of 1853 worked on the Port Erin Breakwater on the Isle of Man. Despite the assertions made by some sources that a locomotive of this type was regauged for use in the Crimea, this would have been highly unlikely as the cranks were located in the gap between the firebox and the inside of the mainframes with the driving axle centred

Below:
Stewarts & Lloyds Minerals 0-6-0ST No 35 was built in 1895; it was photographed on the Foxfield Light Railway on 8 April 1973. *H. S. Gamble*

Above:
Kettering Furnaces No 8 **was a 3ft gauge 0-6-0ST built in 1906. Photographed in Kettering in 1964, it is now in the custody of the Welland Valley Traction Club and can often be seen from Midland main line trains at Market Harborough.** *H. S. Gamble*

Below:
Another Northamptonshire Manning was this 1912-built 0-4-0ST, South Durham Steel & Iron Co's No 14. Shown at Irechester Mines in 1964, it is now to be found at the Northamptonshire Ironstone Railway Trust's Hunsbury Hill site. *H. S. Gamble*

behind the firebox. Regauging would therefore have been an extremely difficult operation and would have entailed a rather radical rebuild.

Before passing on to the next part of the story, it should be noted that E. B. Wilson & Co were not the only manufacturer producing locomotives with the type of boiler under consideration during this period. Boilers of a type similar to *Albion*, the Thwaites locomotive described earlier, were carried by John Hawkshaw's designs on the Lancashire & Yorkshire Railway in the late 1840s (albeit with a different arrangement of safety valves). The Manchester firm of William Fairbairn & Sons produced a series of 2-2-2 well tank locomotives for the 'Little North Western Railway' and other customers during the early 1850s with a boiler virtually identical in design to that used by Wilsons on the Crampton locomotives. One of these locomotives, now named *Baroneza*, is now preserved at the Central Railway of Brazil's workshops in Rio de Janeiro, but according to literature published by the museum there, its cylinders are somewhat larger than the figures quoted by Ahrons for the 'Little North Western' locomotives. As almost exact contemporaries of the Wilson broad gauge locomotives, Longridge & Co of Bedlington, Northumberland, produced four broad gauge 0-4-0 tanks of similar design for use on the Holyhead Breakwater Railway. According to an account in the July 1961 edition of the *Railway Magazine*, one of these locomotives was at that time operating on a similar line at Pontadelgarda on the island of Sao Miguel in the Azores. Some 21 years later this railway was to be very much in the news following the visit there by Colin Garratt, but although he found two much later locomotives still extant, neither he nor any subsequent British visitor appears to have been able to find the Longridge engine.

As regards the evolution of the Manning Wardle standard designs, the next major step as regards the six-coupled type was to come in the year 1853 with the construction by Wilsons of two 0-4-2STs for the Oxford, Worcester & Wolverhampton Railway as their Nos 35 and 36 (E. B. Wilson Works Nos 387 and 388). As David Joy was then the Locomotive Superintendent of this line, and Edward Brown Wilson himself was subsequently to hold this position, the choice of supplier for much of the railway's equipment was not really surprising, but what is more important in the present context is that the close resemblance between the OW&W 0-4-2STs and the later Manning Wardle products is there for all to see. The Ahrons drawing of the Wilson engine clearly shows many of the features which were exhibited by Manning Wardle designs, including the distinctive flat-sided saddle tank, and the closeness of the relationship is further demonstrated by the comparative table of dimensions shown below which includes those of the two most proximate Manning Wardle classes.

Comparative Table of Dimensions

Class:	OW&W No 35	Old 'I'	'K'
Builder:	E. B. Wilson	Manning Wardle	Manning Wardle
Wheel arrangement:	0-4-2	0-6-0	0-6-0
Cylinders:	9¼in×14in	11in×17in	12in×17in
Driving wheels:	3ft 5in	3ft 1⅜in	3ft 1⅜in
Trailing wheels:	3ft 0in		
Wheelbase:	5ft 6in+4ft 9in	5ft 5in+4ft 10in	5ft 5in+5ft 4in
Boiler length:	7ft 0in	7ft 3in	7ft 9in
Boiler diameter:	2ft 9in	2ft 9in	2ft 9in
Firebox wrapper length:	3ft 0in	3ft 0in	3ft 0in
Firebox length:	2ft 5in	?	2ft 5in
Firebox width:	2ft 9in	?	2ft 10¾in
Firebox height:	3ft 4½in	?	3ft 4½in
Tubes:	79@2in	?	78@2in
Weight in working order:	13ton 16cwt	16ton 4cwt	18ton 10cwt

From the dimensions quoted above, it can be seen that, apart from the barrel length, there was little variation in the main boiler dimensions between the three classes. This would appear to be the case notwithstanding the fact that the data for the Manning Wardle Old 'I' class is incomplete, since the maker's drawings for that class were stamped 'class K pattern short boiler'. The total wheelbase of the OW&WR locomotives was the same as that for the Old 'I' design and it can also be seen that there was a mere one inch disparity between the respective positions of the driving axle within that wheelbase. The two OW&WR locomotives have of course long since disappeared (they are both believed to have been scrapped before the turn of the century after sale into industrial service) and, despite some creditable performances of longevity by some of its members, the Old 'I' class is also extinct today. However, the proportions of the original 0-4-2STs can be seen to some extent in the two Manning Wardle 0-6-0STs preserved in Montevideo. Once operated by the Central Railway of Uruguay, there were originally eight locomotives built to this specification and in substance the first three were built to the basic Old 'I' design (and apparently equipped with the classic 'Jenny Lind' type safety valve cover) but with 3ft 6in wheels. The final five, which were all built during the period 1887-1890, used the same dimensions but were turned out in a style more appropriate to their date of construction. For this reason it is clear that the two survivors are from the later series, but what appears less clear is their individual identities. No 42, which stands outside Montevideo station, has been accepted by many enthusiasts as the maker's No 1045 of 1887 (the plate which it carries) but

Above:
An outside cylindered example was *John Robert*, built in 1916 and captured at NCB Birch Coppice in 1965. *H. S. Gamble*

although this number appears on the coupling rods, other parts carry the number 1197. This suggests that the engine is more likely to be works No 1197 of 1890. As for the other locomotive, which still operates school children's specials around the docks, only a few motion parts appear to bear a number at all (this being No 1198). The survival of the 1045 plates and the building date of 1887 attributed to the dock locomotive do suggest, however, that this may be the real No 1045, although the matter remains shrouded in mystery.

Returning once more to events at the Railway Foundry, the final major step towards the evolution of the standard Manning Wardle six-coupled design was to come in 1854 when two small locomotives were delivered to local collieries, one to Waterloo Main (who were later to purchase the Old 'I' type) the other to Denby Grange. The following year, both these locomotives were to achieve an important historical distinction in being purchased by the Government for use on the first military railway in the world. This was the Balaclava line in the Crimea, and reports in the Leeds press described the two locomotives as 0-6-0 saddle tanks with 11in×17in cylinders and 3ft 0in diameter wheels. Unfortunately no drawings or reliable illustrations of them have apparently come to light, but there is some persuasive evidence that the 'double crankpin boss' wheels so prominent on the early Manning Wardle standard locomotives had yet to appear at this stage. A photograph of Worcester Engine Co Works No 1 of 1865, *Salford*, working on the Manchester Ship Canal contract appeared in *Industrial Railway Record* in the mid-1960s, from which it is clear that the design of this locomotive was taken from the same roots. Although the boiler for some reason has a lower firebox casing surmounted by a dome, which at the time would have appeared to be a retrograde step, the plain straight-sided weatherboard and the spaces let into the side sheets to enable satisfactory gripping of the handrails by the crew are more suggestive of the earlier E. B. Wilson influence than of Manning Wardle. The dimensions of the Worcester Engine Co product are slightly larger than the contemporary Old 'I' class with cylinders 11½in×18in and wheels of 3ft 2in diameter, but it is interesting to note that the number of spokes (12) is the same as for the OW&WR 0-4-2 and their design is similar to those on the trailing wheels of that engine. Mainly because of the comparatively late construction of the Worcester Engine Co locomotive, any such inference must be conjectural but it seems likely that the Wilson products sent to the Crimea would have had plain 12-spoke wheels with single crankpin bosses. As regards the compensating levers which linked the spring assemblies on the centre and leading axles on the earlier Manning Wardle six-coupled standard products, it is interesting to note that these had appeared on the Wilson 'Standard Goods' 0-6-0s by 1854 (see the Ahrons illustration of OW&WR No 27) and so it is at least possible that these may have been carried by the Balaclava locomotives.

The standard Manning Wardle four-coupled design would appear to have its roots, rather strangely, in two locomotives with uncoupled wheels supplied for the opening of the first railway in Argentina, the Sociedas del Camino

Left:
***Littleton No 5* was named after the colliery where it worked. Surviving to preservation it was a mainstay of the embryonic Great Central Railway operations at Loughborough.**
H. S. Gamble

de Herro de Buenos Aires al Oueste. This line was a mere six miles long and linked Plaza del Parque in the capital to Floresta. The locomotives (E. B. Wilson Nos 570 and 571 of 1856) carried the names *La Portena* and *La Argentina* and although delivered in mid-1856, opening of the line was delayed by over a year. After withdrawal from service, *La Portena* was preserved at Lujan, some 40 miles from Buenos Aires. Although this locomotive has wheels of 5ft 6in diameter, many of the classic features associated with the early Manning Wardle 0-4-0STs can be seen, including the curvaceous smokebox with lift-up door and the bufferbeams projecting above footplate level. An intriguing feature of *La Portena's* construction is what appears to be a one-piece motion bracket/boiler support assembly which can be noticed immediately behind the leading splasher. This was not a feature repeated on the standard four-coupled classes. The use of the uncoupled wheel configuration on *La Portena* was dictated by necessity as there is insufficient space between the leading wheels and the inside of the crossheads for a coupling rod to pass through.

The historical events leading to the dissolution of E. B. Wilson & Co have been documented elsewhere, but for present purposes all that need be noticed is that former Wilson employees Alexander Campbell, John Manning and Charles Wardle (who had risen to the position of Chief Engineer at the Railway Foundry) became the leading figures in Manning Wardle upon the firm's formation in 1858. The Boyne Engine Works, their premises, were located close to the site of the old Railway Foundry and locomotive construction commenced the following year, which also saw the purchase of some drawings, Lots 3370-3407, from the auction of E. B. Wilson & Co assets. It is known that among the drawings were the designs which were to form the basis of the standard classes, and the first Old 'I' class *Rutland* (Works No 4 of 1859) appeared soon after their purchase. During the firm's 67-year period of locomotive construction, close on 80% of its products officially fell within the standard classifications, although this figure is misleading in that some ostensibly standard locomotives had special features such as domed boilers, whilst many 'specials' were effectively standard in all but name. The designs underwent some alteration over the years: the Wilson feed pumps gave way to injectors, Salter safety valves were replaced by Ramsbottom, the double crankpin bosses disappeared, the saddle tanks became progressively less angular and proper cabs replaced the skimpy weatherboards, but even the last Manning, No 2047 of 1926 (now *Warwickshire* on the Severn Valley Railway) was recognisably out of the original mould. The influence of the Manning Wardle types upon other firms' work could also be seen, particularly in the earlier products of Hunslet Engine Co. When Mannings finally succumbed to economic pressures in 1927, their designs continued to be built by two successive purchasers of their goodwill; their neighbours Kitson & Co and Robert Stephenson & Hawthorns Ltd. The last locomotive of pure Manning Wardle design (RSH No 7032 of 1941) was supplied to Stewarts & Lloyds of Corby as their No 55, and although built some 88 years later, it still showed substantial traces of descent from the Oxford, Worcester & Wolverhampton 0-4-2STs of 1853. For a series of designs built in any numbers, this was truly a remarkable achievement, and outside of the

WARWICKSHIRE

world of preservation, this appears to have been matched in the United Kingdom only in a single isolated instance when the Cannock Chase & Wolverhampton Colliery Co constructed a 0-4-2 locomotive *Foggo* in 1946 to a Beyer Peacock specification of some 90 years vintage.

As far as the United Kingdom preservation scene is concerned, the six-coupled standard designs have fared considerably better than their four-coupled counterparts, and today only one of these latter types can be seen by British enthusiasts at home; No 1795 of 1912 (class 'P') which is preserved by the Northamptonshire Ironstone Trust. Perhaps the greatest tragedy from this point of view was that the historic Wantage Tramway No 7 (1057/1888) was offered to the Kent & East Sussex Railway after withdrawal from industrial service at Cordes Steel Mills in Newport for the princely sum of £80. However, the line's need at that time for workable locomotives militated against the Wantage engine (which required a new boiler) and she was cut up in 1964.

The career of the Bluebell Line's *Sharpthorn* is perhaps typical of early Manning Wardle products. She was outshopped to the order of C. Decon of Kettering as a 'K' class locomotive bearing the name *Solomon*. After a mere one year's usage, she was sold to the contractor J. Firbank for use on the construction of the LBSCR's Lewes-East Grinstead line, thereby establishing her historical connection with the Bluebell Railway and acquiring her present name. After passing through the hands of W. Rigby of Duffield, who renamed her *Jessie*, she was acquired by Samuel Williams & Co of Dagenham Docks in 1889 from the dealer, C. D. Phillips of Newport. Whilst at Dagenham, the locomotive became just plain *Samuel Williams No 4* and she not only shared her accommodation with other Manning Wardle specimens but also with the erstwhile Hunslet Engine Co No 1 of 1865, which eventually became another unfortunate 'near-miss' as regards preservation. As their No 4, *Sharpthorn* gave Samuel Williams some 69 years of useful service and she even received a radio telephone in 1954. Some four years later the engine was withdrawn, and after three years of static display at Dagenham, she was loaned to Bressingham Hall, Diss. At around this time, the Bluebell showed considerable interest in the idea of outright purchase of the locomotive from Samuel Williams and the necessary approaches were made, but main line acquisitions took priority at this stage and so matters rested there until Samuel Williams themselves regained possession of the locomotive in 1981. *Sharpthorn* duly returned on loan to the line she helped to build in time for its centenary in 1982 but the purchase negotiations were complicated by Samuel Williams' liquidation. A figure of £1,500 was eventually agreed with the liquidator however, with the result that the acquisition finally took place some 22 years after it was first envisaged.

Preliminary estimates have put the cost of *Sharpthorn's* restoration to working order at some £6,000, mostly accounted for by materials, but as no records came with the locomotive from Samuel Williams, the full extent of the work has yet to be ascertained, although considerable boiler and firebox repairs are anticipated. In any case, because of higher priority items on the agenda, it is estimated that the necessary repairs will be delayed for approximately five years, but it is hoped that *Sharpthorn* will be available for at least a ceremonial role in the future reconstruction of the Horsted Keynes-East Grinstead section. For the present, those wishing to see an example of a working representative of the Manning Wardle standard designs should visit the South Cambridgeshire Railway near Royston, which boasts *Newcastle* (1532/1901), a beautifully restored 'M' class, although prior written permission *must* be obtained for such a visit. Notwithstanding the scarcity of working examples, however, the contribution made to Britain's railway history as a whole by Manning Wardle and its products should never be overlooked.

Top left:
The last Manning was turned out for the Rugby Portland Cement Co Ltd in 1926; it was their No 4. It was working at the Cement Co's New Bilton Works when photographed on 23 March 1966. *H. S. Gamble*

Bottom left:
No 4 is preserved on the Severn Valley Railway, being amongst the first locomotives to arrive at Bridgnorth. It is seen there, carrying the name *Warwickshire*, on 16 May 1971. *H. S. Gamble*

The author would like to thank Dr Paul E. Waters of the British Overseas Railways Historical Trust for the information on the Uruguayan locomotives, and Klaus Marx of the Bluebell Railway for the information on *Sharpthorn*.

You Have Been Warned!

P. Butler

In recent years there has been an increasing awareness of the dangers and stupidity of trespassing on the railway. This is usually the work of a small group of photographers intent on getting a different angle on a special train or locomotive. I won't belabour the point but it did set me thinking about what lengths earlier railway companies went to, in order to point out to the general public that trespassing was an offence, and that it carried heavy penalties.

I have, over the years in my travels, photographed 'trespass' signs, so I dug through my collection and found that mainly they were either from the Midland Railway or the North Eastern Railway.

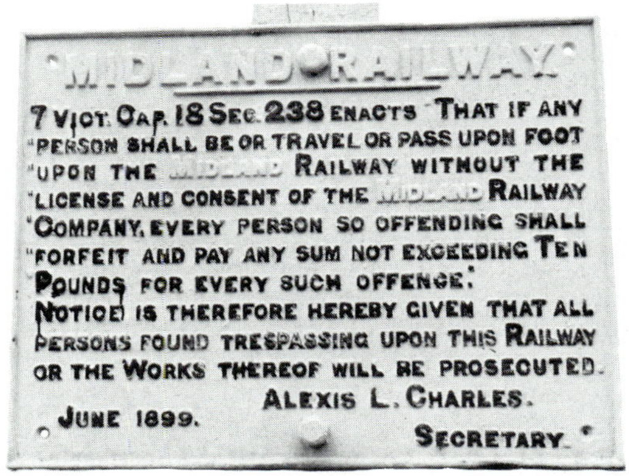

The 1899 version coincided with Charles's appointment as Secretary in June that year. It was photographed in 1968. *P. E. B. Butler*

A Midland Railway sign dated 1893 at Ribblehead station in 1971. *P. E. B. Butler*

Taking a little time to study the two groups of photographs, several things became apparent, which at first sight might not seem that important. Firstly, the notices of these two pre-Grouping companies were signed by the company secretaries rather than the general manager. Most histories of companies tell you about the general manager, what he was like, how he treated the staff, etc, but rarely does the secretary get a mention. My own researches, plus help from the NRM at York, left me with what I believe to be a complete list of secretaries for both companies. These are set out in the table, and show the names and the years when they held office.

Secondly, both sets of signs seem to have appeared at about the same time — Williams appearing on the scene in 1868 and Wilkinson in 1871. Was this a new departure for all the companies or did the railways have earlier generations of trespass warning notices? Possibly in the early days with slow, and not too frequent trains, no one took much notice of lineside walkers, but with the passage of time had come faster trains and possibly an increase in fatalities and the nuisance value of trespassers.

The third point that made me stop and think was the difference in penalties and the value of them. Note that the Midland talked about sums '. . . up to ten pounds', whilst the NER had a flat rate of 40 shillings (£2). You would be paid very well if you commanded a wage of £1 a week in those far-off days. If one scales it up to today's average wage of circa £150, then the minimum fine today would be £300 and the maximum £1,500, taking the Midland's highest figure! Of course, what I do not

Left:
Another plate commemorating Secretary Charles but dated 1906. Photographed on the Up side at Fiskerton Junction in 1985. *P. E. B. Butler*

Above:
A North Eastern Railway sign seen near Arthington in 1972. Wilkinson served from 1871 to 1903. *P. E. B. Butler*

Below:
Dunnell was the last NER secretary, serving from 1905 until 1922. This specimen was recorded at Haltwhistle in 1973. *P. E. B. Butler*

know is how often the companies took people to court for trespassing alone, where no damage, theft or vandalism was involved.

Be that as it may, they went to great trouble to produce these signs by the thousands and to install and maintain them. Note that in the case of the NER sign photographed at Battersby, a special casting has been made and fixed over the old name. It would be interesting to know whose name was underneath. Common sense dictates that it would be Wilkinson since it is doubtful if Wedgwood's short tenure of office would have been long enough for his name to be immortalised in cast iron!

Turning to the LNER sign from Crianlarich, we find that our company secretary

Top:
A re-cycled North Eastern sign at Batterby Junction in 1971.
P. E. B. Butler

Above right:
An anonymous LNER sign at Crianlarich in 1970.
P. E. B. Butler

Right:
There cannot have been many cast iron signs naming the British Transport Commission, and very few of them can have been mounted on bridge rail as appears to have been the case here at Blatchbridge Junction, Frome. The photograph was taken in 1980. *Spencer W. Hall*

has given way to an anonymous BY ORDER. A move towards the faceless, nameless, unaccountable civil servant of today, perhaps! Note too that no specific sum of money is mentioned and that imprisonment is now a possibility!

So to our final examples, namely those of the British Transport Commission. The old cast iron sign from Frome takes us back to the fixed sum of two pounds (40 shillings) but with a promise of a month in prison if you fail to pay up. The smaller enamel example is/was fixed to one of the legs of the support structure for the signalbox at Northumberland Park at the country end of the up platform. This was photographed in November 1985 and shows that if one keeps one's eyes open, such little gems from our railways' earlier days are still there to be photographed and recorded.

So the next time you are tempted to trespass, stop and think — perhaps you might do better to photograph that old trespass sign rather than that 'Castle' or Class 40 which will have been photographed a thousand times already that day!

Secretaries of the North Eastern Railway

Captain William O'Brien	1854-1856
John Cleghorn	1856-1870
Christopher Newman Wilkinson	1871-1903
Ralph Lewis Wedgwood	1904-1905
Robert Francis Dunnell	1905-1922

Secretaries of the Midland Railway

J. F. Bell	1844-1853
Joseph Sanders	1853-1856
G. N. Browne	1857-1868
J. Moore (appointed *pro tem* 1 July 1868)	
James Williams	1868-1899
Alexis Leon Charles	1899-1916
W. N. Bancroft	1916-1923

Below:
The enamel BTC sign is more in keeping with its period. This example was seen at Northumberland Park in 1985. *P. E. B. Butler*

The 'Cambridge Connection'

1

Allan Garraway

Virtually at the booked time a gleaming diesel and its train of special coaches appear under the distant bridge and slowly roll around the sharp curve. As it enters the station there is just time to take a quick photograph before grabbing my bag ready to board. The platform is short and the train a long main line one, not usual on this line, so I guess that I shall have to board where it stops and walk through to wherever my seat has been allocated. Coach by coach, the train rolls slowly past until I am left watching its receding tail lamp. And this is a train which I have been specially invited to travel on, having already travelled some 500 miles to do so!

The 5 May 1986 special from Cambridge to Stratford-upon-Avon, the 'Cambridge Connection' had been one of Michael Seymour's fine ideas. It was named to mark the connection which exists between the Festiniog Railway (celebrating its 150th anniversary in 1985) and Cambridge University and town, at a time when the University Railway Club was celebrating its 75th anniversary. Festiniog officers Alan Pegler, John Routly, The Earl of Lindsay, Trevor Bailey, Dick Hardy, Michael and I all had connections with either town, gown or Railway Club. It was also an occasion to mark the end of my own active connection with the FR.

Some months beforehand Mike Seymour had telephoned to see if I would join them and I had very readily agreed, particularly as the steam power was to be that great favourite of mine, *Sir Nigel Gresley*. I did, however, ask Mike to confirm the details as quickly as possible, as I could see problems in finding a convenient boarding point on a Bank Holiday Monday morning; he assured me that there would be a stop in the London area. With bitter experience of late running, I asked Aviemore to book a sleeper on the early train for me, but when I called to collect my ticket I found that they were still holding my application, as there was advice that due to engineering works all Anglo-Scottish trains would be about 1½ hours late. Further enquiries revealed that West Coast services were being diverted over the Settle & Carlisle

Below:
Allan Garraway with No 4498 *Sir Nigel Gresley* at Bicester on 5 May 1986. *Michael Seymour*

line, the one which BR says it does not use and wants to close; additionally, I was told to expect even longer delays. As it was still impossible to obtain precise timings, I consulted BR's steam supremo David Ward, who advised leaving earlier and travelling via the East Coast.

As is always the way when a little delay is of no consequence, a deserted and otherwise closed King's Cross was reached early. A walk down Euston Road found Euston station almost equally asleep, but at least there was a snack bar open and I was able to get a cuppa and a sandwich. The sleeper had given the option of a very early call with a tea tray or a little longer sleep — I had gone for the 'lie in'.

I had agreed to join the special at Willesden High Level, where it was booked to stop for a minute at 09.25. Although it was also booked to change engines at West Ruislip, I was attracted by the prospect of the unusual wander from the North London line to the West of England main line and thence up to the Birmingham line via Greenford. The depths of Euston suburban and thence the run out to Willesden made a change, another station to look at, and from the High Level there was at least some railway activity to see. A succession of sleeper trains went through one after another, one being the early Inverness so it was a good thing that I had travelled as I had.

The Willesden High Level platforms are now only three coaches long, situated on a sharp curve with a 10mph speed restriction, so that as the train ground its way through, with Michael and the others looking out and waving. I was not concerned until I realised that the last coach was passing and that the train was not stopping. As the train slowly rolled over the West Coast main line bridge

Below:
Participants on the occasion of the 'Cambridge Connection': left to right, *front*, D. R. Pepperell, co-organiser, CRC; Michael Seymour, co-organiser, Archivist FR Co, Vice-President CURC; Allan Garraway; Alan Pegler, Cambridge University, President FR Co and FRSL; Trevor Bailey, CURC, Trustee FR Trust; Les Smith, Director FR Co; *on locomotive*, Julian Riddick, A4 Locomotive Society; Barry Moore, co-organiser CRC. *R. Clarke*

and veered right at the junction, many thoughts passed through my mind. Would they be able to stop the train for Me? How would I be able to get on? What were my chances of getting a taxi to get me to West Ruislip in time? Why had the train not stopped? I have been at barriers or platforms and seen trains start away just as I got to them, but never have I been on a platform waiting for a train which failed to stop as expected.

Fortunately the train was stopped some distance further on and under BR staff supervision I was able to join it.

Apparently it had taken time for Mike to find the guard and get him to stop the train; they later found that the driver did not have a Willesden stop on his working sheet. However, I was aboard. The guard gave the 'right away' and a cup of coffee and conversations with old colleagues soon started a very memorable day. The run in to West Ruislip alongside *Sir Nigel Gresley* was a rare pleasure. After Dick Hardy had fired up the bank through Saunderton, I had the pleasure of doing the same on to Bicester. An excellent lunch was had, followed by some sightseeing at Stratford. The return journey, with so many East Anglians to talk to, was going well until the diesel came on again at West Ruislip and the driver decided to change over to air brakes. He did not release them properly at first and by the time we got to Ealing he had ruined two sets of wheels — a coach was detached there, depriving us of an hour of daylight. Many had travelled some distance to join the special at Cambridge and did not appreciate the considerable delay which ensued. Nevertheless, Mike Seymour and his friends are to be congratulated for making such a great connection.

Below:
BR Standard '78000' class 2-6-0 No 78013 heads a Cambridge University Railway Club 'engine driving special', a regular club event in steam days, away from Edmondthorpe & Wymondham station in October 1965. *V. L. Murphy*

2

R. H. N. Hardy

Any journey over the Great Central Section of the LNER was interesting, absorbing and sometimes very exciting indeed; a hilly and dashing railway via the 'Met' and scarcely less so via the GW&GC Joint, the 'New Line' as it was called. Sadly one cannot nowadays reach Stratford-upon-Avon via Aylesbury, Woodford Halse and the 'Nibble & Clink', nor even by Aylesbury unless you go backwards to Princes Risborough, so I doubt if we shall ever see an LNER 'A4' Pacific climbing once more to Amersham and dashing down the other side through the woodlands and off the edge of the Chilterns on to the Vale of Aylesbury. Once more? Oh yes, just now and again they were allowed on the route for odd trips, but it was mostly the original 'A1' Pacifics, later rebuilt to Class A3.

Since I joined the LNER early in 1941, I have covered many thousands of miles on the Gresley Pacifics but never did I think that I would work my passage on No 4498 *Sir Nigel Gresley* up the 'Long Drag' from Appleby to Ais Gill, nor from time to time between Marylebone and Stratford-upon-Avon. I had known this wonderful machine before, having worked on her when she was a real 'stuma' during the war (a journey I remember only too well) and later, when she was booked to Driver William Hoole, of whom I have to say that he had a certain reputation as a chimney wobbler but, fit as I was in those days, I did not find him unduly merciless!

So on 5 May 1986 I was once more on the old engine, for what I think was to be my fifth journey from Marylebone on it in recent times. I travelled to Marylebone to pick up the locomotive and support coach along with Julian Riddick and the splendid gang from the North who not only look after the engine but keep Julian in order as well. Marylebone is a DMU depot with no second men stationed there, so both driver and fireman booked for

Above:
No 60007 *Sir Nigel Gresley* leaves Edinburgh with the 10.30 SO for Aberdeen on 17 July 1965. *Paul Riley*

the job have long since been passed out and appointed drivers. Normally the younger men who were not passed on steam as drivers do the firing, but on this occasion our crew were Brian Axtell and Gerry Wood, both in their 50s and both qualified steam drivers.

It is a long time since some depots had the 'too old at 40' links into which men could go if they felt that everyday firing on the main line was getting too much for them, but the older one gets the more one uses one's head to save one's body. Brian was a Neasden man, having started there in August 1949. By that time promotion was very brisk and he was old enough to be passed for firing duties in May 1950. After National Service and firing on all classes of work he was passed for driving in June 1960. During the next 22 months he had a great deal of driving experience which would not have come his way at many depots. The weekend 'Starlight Specials' to Leicester were frequently worked by spare men and were a fair assignment with a Pacific, 'Green Arrow' or 'B1' for a young crew. But main line work soon puts an old head on young shoulders. He went across to Cricklewood for his driver's check in 1962 and back to Marylebone in February 1965, for the end of steam on the Great Central section. Brian would sit up in his corner absorbed in his job, never for a moment having to watch his fireman's work, for he could feel how things were without looking.

I had always thought Gerry Wood had done his work at Neasden — a compliment to him for he was very much at home on No 4498 back in February 1985 when I first made a journey with him. In fact he started at Willesden in 1953 and did all his firing over there before being passed for driving in May 1962. He came across to Marylebone for his check in 1967 and has stayed ever since. Very much at home as a driver and fireman on No 4498, he has nonetheless a very soft spot for that Big Red Engine from 'over the other side'.

Our Inspector was Owen Edgington who had come to Marylebone from Saltley, Birmingham, via the Southern Region at Waterloo. Owen, who is now Train Crew Manager at Cambridge, had matters very much in hand, quietly and firmly, essential characteristics required of an Inspector; on the road unobtrusive but ever present and effective.

The supervision of two experienced and competent men, one of whom has the total responsibility for handling locomotive and train, is an art that can only be acquired by experience and above all by the tactful projection of personality.

I seem to remember that I was allowed through to the locomotive somewhere about Denham and worked my passage to High Wycombe. Mike Seymour of the Festiniog Railway had expressed a wish to see my creaking bones in action, so he had his opportunity and when we passed High Wycombe such was the freedom of steam production that I did not immediately pick up the shovel. Gerry took this as a dual opportunity of showing his own capability up Saunderton bank, giving me a rest I did not need, for rarely does a fireman get tired over the GC on No 4498, which steams on a candle. I watched Gerry at work, a London Midland fireman with a technique different to ours but equally effective, as we climbed to Saunderton steadily and firmly, and maybe faster than the 'Kings', 'Castles' and Pacifics before the war. But there were no excesses from Brian, consistent enginemanship with all adjustments gently and imperceptibly made. I could not tell the speed we were doing up the bank, our work was concerned with steam, water, fire and the avoidance of smoke and waste of steam on the easy stretch after the summit. A perfect, consistent journey, very nicely done by all concerned.

Coming back from Stratford we had on two Leamington drivers, both Western men who had grown to admire and respect the 'A4'. Vic Waters, who started at Barry, and Graham White, who started at Leamington, becoming a driver there after a spell at Coventry, were both in their early 50s. Both had experience of LNER, LMSR and SR engines as well as their own. The Inspector, Arthur Cosmett, originated from Saltley and he became a driver at Monument Lane, Aston, and New Street before being promoted Inspector. He was back to steam after a long period on diesel traction.

It is not always realised how different are the techniques required on the locomotives of different railways. The Great Western engines were normally fired down the middle of a long narrow firebox, the coal being thrown into a large heap whence it shuffled or was drawn to the sides and front of the grate. The firehole door was large and the shovel even larger. To an Eastern man this shovel was a detestable dung-spreading implement, to the iron-muscled Western man it was just the job. An 'A4' requires the coal to be placed through a small firehole door far into the rear corners, along the sides and into the front corners with very little in the centre

and under the door where an excess of coal will prevent the proper use of the wrists in twisting the narrow-bladed light shovel for back corner firing. This is completely different to a GW engine, as is every fitting on the firebox front — regulator, reversing gear, vacuum brake, injectors, gauge frames and glasses. It is not so easy to tackle a strange locomotive as some would think, and yet before traction training became standard practice with the new forms of locomotion, men were expected to step on to a strange engine and get going, by night or daylight.

Our Western friends were on top of the job and when I went through, Vic Waters was performing with full regulator and 15% cut off, steam and water just so, very nicely done. And so to Banbury, where the old firm are waiting on the platform. Trevor Barnett and Mick Holloway had the 'A4' when it first came to Marylebone in 1985 and over the years had done a fair bit on the West Somerset to keep their hands in. With them is Peter Witt, Traction Inspector. Peter came from Camden where he had done Carlisle, Liverpool, Manchester and Lodge many times as a fireman and as an 'extra link' driver. In this way young men had a varied experience covering a wide variety of work, a standard arrangement at most of the ex-LNWR sheds. As a result he had a few miles under his belt before he came to Marylebone as a driver, where he gained valuable route knowledge. And now he is as much at home on an 'A4' as he was on those LMS locomotives out of Euston, and he keeps very much in touch.

Above:
The second run of the 'Cambridge Connection' took place on 11 May 1986, when it was photographed approaching High Wycombe. *Hugh Ballantyne*

As to Trevor, he started at Tyseley in January 1953, doing both firing and driving there until he was made redundant as a young driver in October 1968. He managed

Left:
Dick Hardy wielding the shovel on *Sir Nigel Gresley* on 5 May 1986. *R. H. N. Hardy collection*

to get in at Marylebone, a move he never regretted, although he never dreamed that he would be driving an 'A4' as a result! I happen to have come across one or two who knew him as a fireman; they say he was very good. How he manipulated those GW shovels is a mystery to me, but you do not have to be a big man to be a good and skilful fireman. Trevor lives for railway work and he handles a Gresley Pacific as it was designed to be worked — calmly and predictably.

And then Mick Holloway, who started at Watford in 1962, became a Willesden fireman six months later and transferred to Marylebone in 1964. He saw steam out and in the process fired for some of the best Neasden drivers, who had many years of experience and who gave great thought and care to their work in the difficult last days of steam. So now a steam locomotive of high quality is exactly Mick's cup of tea, as can be seen when he is at work, neither making smoke nor wasting steam.

A happy day — many old friends from Cambridge on the train, including Bill Last who cleaned the then recently transferred 'D16s' Nos 8783 and 8787, the famous Royal engines. Also present was Les Smith of the Festiniog Railway Co board, associated with the 'A4' Pacifics since they were built, living as he did on the Great Northern section; and Allan Garraway, of course, a guest like myself. A one-time King's Lynn fireman, the home of Bill Bowyer whom I knew when I was at Lynn in the middle 1940s, I met him quite by chance on the train and neither of us had forgotten anything or anyone over the intervening years.

Thus was railway work: one knew thousands of men of whose memory time never deals harshly. In this connection, perhaps I can be permitted to close with a Liverpool Lime Street story.

Not long ago I travelled from Runcorn to Euston and as we went along the driver said to me 'Mr Hardy, you must have known an awful lot of railway men in your time'.

'Oh yes,' I replied, 'I suppose I've known very well indeed about 25,000 over the years, maybe more.'

Most men would have said something about the considerable number, and asked how my memory coped with it, but not my Liverpudlian. Quick as a flash came the reply: 'Arhh, you'll have a good funeral, den.'

This is the joy of footplate work; laughter and fun march side by side with competence and dedication as on the 48-year-old *Sir Nigel Gresley* on the GC (and GW) main line.

Above:
Pushing coal forward at Stratford on 5 May 1986.
M. Seymour

Footnote by Michael Seymour, Archivist of the FR Co

The idea of the 'Cambridge Connection' was born on 22 January 1985 when I had my trip on the Post Office Train Stamps VSOE Special to Didcot. I had hoped for No 4472 from Cambridge to perhaps Doncaster and points north, but David Ward scotched that, so the Cambridge-London-Stratford route was settled on and agreed with David. I thought we were going to fail in finding enough customers for one train on 5 May but in the event the demand justified a second run on 11 May. The connection was firstly to celebrate Allan Garraway's years with the FR Co, then to mark the link between the FR and Cambridge, that year being the 75th anniversary of the CURC (as far as I know, the third oldest railway club in the country, though it was formed as a branch of the Railway Club — the oldest). Incidentally the first commercial train hauled by an 'A4' was by No 2509 *Silver Link*, King's Cross-Cambridge on 14 September 1935, the morning 'Parliamentary', before the first 'Silver Jubilee' run. No 4498 was thus an appropriate choice of motive power. The CURC has an original *Silver Link* nameplate, given by Sir Nigel Gresley.

'Leicester Gap' Signalboxes

The 'Leicester Gap' is the name given to the section of the Midland main line from Wellingborough to Loughborough, which until 1986 was still operated by traditional semaphore signalling controlled by 24 manual signalboxes. On either side of this stretch, multiple-aspect colour light signalling was in operation; controlled by Trent power signalbox in the north and West Hampstead box in the south.

With the commissioning of a new £30 million power signalbox at Leicester, the long-serving and outdated semaphore boxes and signals could finally be taken out of use, and their distinctive outlines disappeared for ever, to leave just five power signalboxes to control the Midland main line between St Pancras and Sheffield.

All photographs by Mike Haddon

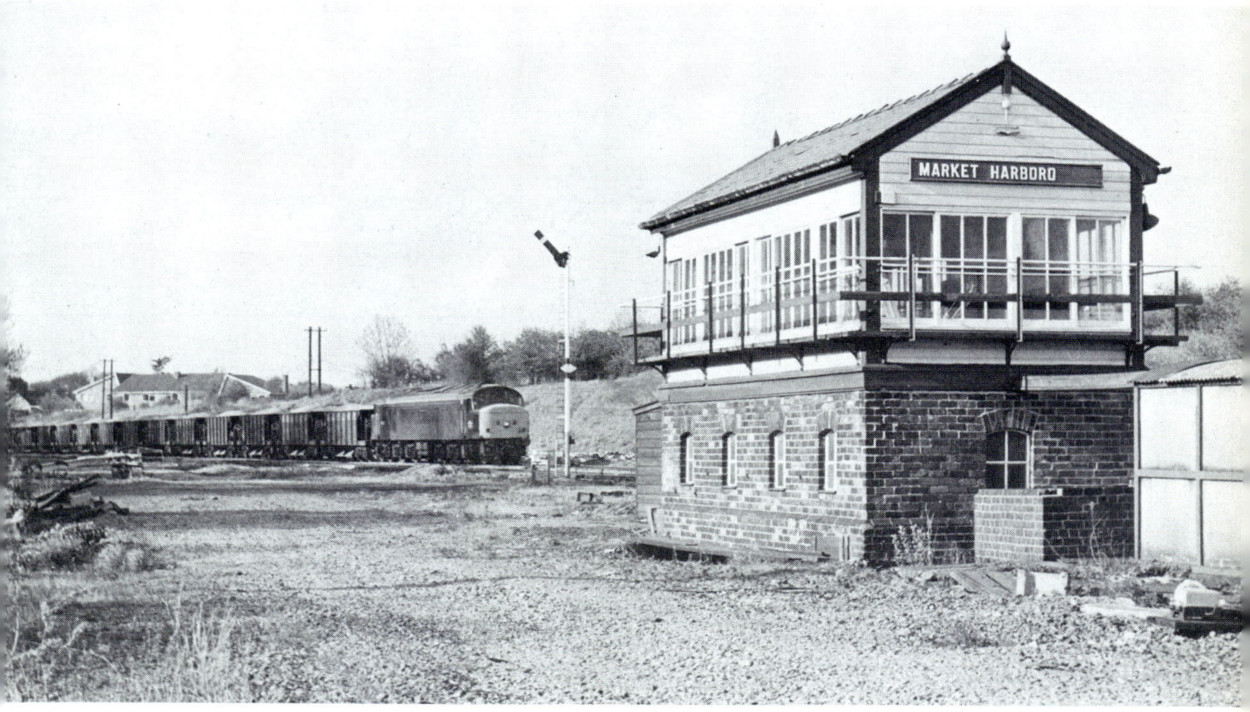

Above:
Market Harborough. Despite controlling a section of the Midland main line, this box was built by the LNWR and actually faced the trackbed (in the foreground) of that company's line to Northampton. It was photographed on 12 May 1986.

Top:
East Langton, north of Market Harborough, is seen on 23 April 1986.

Above right:
Kibworth Station was a particularly unusual box, having lost its pitched roof as a result of fire damage.

Right:
Kilby Bridge signalbox south of Wigston was unusual because of its pedestal. This box has been preserved by the Midland Railway Trust.

Above:
Wigston South Junction, like the others, has now been demolished or removed. It stood in front of a row of Midland Railway cottages and is seen on 12 May 1986.

Below:
Wigston North Junction signalbox, also on 12 May 1986.

Top:
London Road Junction, Leicester, must have been the most difficult to photograph. Class 31 No 31417 passes with the 09.30 Ipswich-Birmingham on 12 May 1986.

Above:
No 31282 on parcels duty passes Leicester North on 23 April 1986. The new signalling centre is on the right.

Right:
The attractive signalbox of typical Midland Railway design at Sileby, south of Loughborough, seen on 11 May 1986.

The British Travelling Post Office 1985/86

Peter Johnson

When *The British Travelling Post Office* was published by Ian Allan in February 1985, the TPO network had been reasonably static for several years and it was expected that the only changes likely to occur in the foreseeable future would relate to the withdrawal of some minor services. This has proved not to be the case, for although TPOs have been withdrawn from most of the East Coast route, elsewhere there have been positive developments, including the introduction of an experimental service and, on two occasions, temporary services. Additionally the Post Office's public relations officers have discovered the attraction of the TPOs to the media as will be seen. The events and changes are described here in date order. Some further notes are appended concerning other matters on which new information has come to light since the book was published.

For seven weeks from 3 June 1985 most of Crewe station was closed whilst the track layout was modernised, with most services diverted away whilst the work was carried out. Mail handling was transferred to Stafford with TPOs calling there instead of Crewe. The one exception was the York-Shrewsbury TPO which by-passed Stafford. To cover this omission a temporary service was introduced based on Shrewsbury, the Shrewsbury-Stafford Sorting Carriage, which was conveyed to Stafford in company with the Shrewsbury-York and Cardiff-Crewe TPOs, possibly the only time that three TPOs have run in one train. The return duty, the Stafford-Shrewsbury SC, was worked to Shrewsbury with the Crewe-Cardiff TPO. Rubber datestamps were issued for the temporary services, with the regular datestamps remaining in use on the other services affected. Despite it operating for seven weeks, enthusiasts did not become aware of the temporary service and its datestamps until well into July, so covers, despite their philatelic interest, are scarce.

During 1985 the Post Office celebrated its 350th anniversary with functions through-

Left:
Eddie McKee sorting and labelling bags on the Whitehaven-Huddersfield TPO in carriage No 80329 on 5 September 1985.
Peter Johnson

out the country. The North Western Postal Board made its contribution on 5 September, when it arranged for ex-LMS Class 5 4-6-0 No 4767 *George Stephenson* to haul the Whitehaven-Huddersfield TPO as far as Carnforth. A press party was taken from Manchester by a special train, hauled by Class 40 D200, which was attached to the TPO stock at Workington, allowing access to the TPO operations for interviewing, filming and photography. Being late away from Barrow-in-Furness, postal officials tried to calculate the last occasion that a TPO was reported late because of the engine taking water, as it was on this occasion! The press left the train at Manchester Victoria.

A major reorganisation of part of the TPO network took place later the same month, when all services were withdrawn between King's Cross and York and between Newcastle and Edinburgh. The London-York-Edinburgh, the Edinburgh-York and the Edinburgh portion of the North Eastern were withdrawn after the night of 27 September. From 30 September the following changes were made:

North Eastern TPO rerouted to operate between St Pancras and Newcastle via Derby. The late box at King's Cross was closed and a notice installed at St Pancras advising prospective posters to post on the train during the hour it stands in the platform before departure.

Midland TPO truncated, to operate between Bristol and Derby, connecting with the North Eastern TPO there.

Crewe-Peterborough TPO diverted to run via Grantham instead of Leicester, the North Eastern Up making a compensatory stop at Leicester.

Crewe-Peterborough TPO (Lincoln Section) also diverted via Grantham.

The purpose of these changes was to take advantage of the opportunities offered by using Derby as an interchange between the different means of transport.

A minor extension was made to the network on 20 January 1986 when the Chester Relief Sorting Carriage was introduced on an experimental basis. This operates from Chester to Crewe and back at the same times as the former Bangor-Crewe (and reverse) TPO. Its purpose is to handle mail coming off the other TPOs at Crewe bound for North Wales, which were previously taken into Chester Sorting Office. Most of the work is carried out whilst the carriage is platformed at Crewe; an improved North Wales delivery is given as a result. A steel datestamp was issued and is authorised for use on late mail by TPO Section although there appears to be some confusion about this by the Chester men who work the duty.

Above:
The inside view of the famous TPO letter box, also on No 80329. *Peter Johnson*

In February 1986 British Rail undertook the replacement of Proof House bridges just south of Birmingham New Street station. For a nine-day period, including two weekends, trains were diverted whilst the work was carried out. This resulted in the following changes to TPO services for the five nights commencing 24 February:

Left:
Bill Cockburn and Class 47/4 No 47515 *Night Mail* at Derby on 25 September 1986.
Peter Johnson

Below left:
Sorting on the North Eastern TPO Night Up on the morning of 26 September 1986.
Peter Johnson

The North Western Night Down and the Up and Down Special TPOs were routed via Tamworth.

The Midland TPO was routed via Camp Hill in each direction.

A temporary TPO ran between Birmingham and Worcester where it joined up with the Derby-Bristol TPO, this arrangement also operating in the reverse direction. On at least one occasion the Birmingham-Worcester portion was late and ran through to Bristol as a separate train, and on one or two nights the connection was made at Gloucester instead of Worcester. The Birmingham portion was considered to be the main TPO so temporary rubber datestamps were issued to the Derby portion.

A Birmingham Section of the Up and Down Specials connected with those services at Crewe. Rubber datestamps were issued.

A Birmingham Section of the North Western TPO ran from Euston, being issued with a rubber datestamp. It returned to London as the Birmingham-London Bag Tender. A rubber datestamp was issued and used, mainly on philatelic mail, but its usage was probably prompted by the posting of commercial mail at Birmingham — the Post Office omitted to withdraw the late posting facility.

Bag tenders also operated between Birmingham and Derby twice each night and between Birmingham and Longbridge. No datestamps were issued for these.

The grapevine was fully functional on this occasion and postings were made throughout the week, the postal officers proving to be most co-operative.

The film *Night Mail* was made in 1936, being widely acclaimed and remaining popular with a wide audience through the years. In 1986 the Post Office commissioned a revised version to show how the mail handling network has been modernised, using air and road as well as rail. A set of six mail carriages (Nos 80365, 80422, 80320, 80362, 80421, 80363) and brake van No 80868 were repainted from blue and grey to the present Post Office livery of red with yellow lettering, for a filming run made on Saturday 20 September 1986. The special ran from Cricklewood sidings to Leicester and back, covering the Wellingborough-Leicester section twice. Further stock is to be turned out in this livery as it becomes due for repainting.

The film's 50th anniversary was celebrated on 25 September 1986 when Mr Bill Cockburn, the Post Office's Managing Director Letters, named Class 47 locomotive No 47515 *Night Mail*; more filming took place on this occasion, the completed film being broadcast, with the original, on Channel 4 on 3 January 1987. After the naming and a visit to the nearby East Midlands Airport to see the mail-handling there, the locomotive took the North Eastern TPO Night Up to London. A small party of journalists, accommodated in a buffet car attached to the red postal set, conducted interviews en route. No 47515 was also to work the Down North Eastern the following night.

Further insight into TPO operations, as applied to the North Eastern TPO, were obtained from Newcastle-based Assistant Inspector Ken Redpath. The TPO left Newcastle with 44 men on board, 16 of whom transferred to the Midland TPO at Derby, travelling as far as Birmingham, whilst the remaining 28 worked through to St Pancras. The reverse occurred in the down direction, with 16 men joining from the Midland TPO at Derby. The junior men of the team open the bags, remove the registered letters and empty the bags on to the sorting desk; this enables them to learn the routines by observation. The registered letters are dealt with by the senior man on duty. On the subject of seniority, it is interesting that TPO men do not value their pre-TPO service; Ken Redpath refused to talk of anything but his 20 years on TPOs and Wilf Martin, his clerk, took a couple of minutes to calculate that he had a total of 22 years' service, of which 17 were on TPOs. Two men deal with Datapost (for which two datestamps are issued) as far as Derby, reflecting the traffic that the East Midlands Airport generates. A third datestamp is spare. On a normal night about 800 bags of mail are dealt with on the Up; sometimes 1,000 bags are handled, a heavy night's work, although usual for the Down. Refreshment breaks are not scheduled and may only be taken if the work is finished — we did see a couple of enormous teapots being carried through the train as we approached St Pancras and the atmosphere was noticeably more relaxed. Even when the destination is reached — early on this occasion — there is still another hour's work to be done before the lodgings can be sought.

TPOs became the centre of media attention again on 26 September 1986, when the Post Office launched its Capital Letters scheme to speed delivery of first class letters between London and 20 major towns and cities, using air, road and rail transport. Sir Ron Dearing, Chairman of the Post Office, named Class 47 locomotive No 47549 *Royal Mail* at St Pancras. The locomotive, carrying a headboard, 'The Flying Postman', then took invited guests to Bedford and back in a train which had three of the red mail coaches (80365, 80422, 80320) attached. To demonstrate a TPO at work, a quantity of second class mail bound for Yorkshire had been loaded aboard and was sorted for the visitors on the return journey after lunch had been taken. Only first class mail and Datapost is normally carried on TPOs and, being of a time sensitive nature, could not be used for demonstration purposes; hence the use of second class mail. The guests were later given a Hornby model mail coach (complete with now obsolete exchange apparatus) customised in current Post Office livery, and a souvenir cover cancelled with a reserve North Eastern Down TPO datestamp.

Current TPO Services

Only those services which have seen major change since *The British Travelling Post Office* was published are listed.

Chester Relief Sorting Carriage
Chester (dep 23.00)-Crewe (arr 23.27, dep 02.50)-Chester (arr 03.11). Stock stabled at Holyhead.

Crewe-Peterborough Travelling Post Office
Crewe (dep 00.43)-Stoke-on-Trent-Derby

'Black 5' on the mail: No 44767 *George Stephenson* in the bay at Workington, with spare postal stock alongside, prior to working the Whitehaven-Huddersfield TPO on 5 September 1985.
Peter Johnson

TPO Network. *Post Office*

(arr 01.55, dep 02.10)-Nottingham-Grantham-Peterborough (arr 03.53). Lincoln Section detached at Grantham. Stock stabled at Peterborough.

Crewe-Peterborough Travelling Post Office (Lincoln Section)
Grantham (dep 03.21)-Lincoln (arr 04.10). Detached from the Crewe-Peterborough TPO at Grantham. Stock stabled at Lincoln.

Edinburgh-York Travelling Post Office
Ceased 27 September 1985.

London-York-Edinburgh Travelling Post Office
Ceased 27 September 1985.

Midland Travelling Post Office Going North
Bristol (dep 19.35)-Gloucester-Birmingham (arr 21.46, dep 22.40)-Derby (arr 23.37). One carriage transferred to the North Eastern TPO Down at Derby. Stock returns to Bristol as Midland TPO Going South.

Midland Travelling Post Office Going South
Derby (dep 00.40)-Birmingham (arr 01.28, dep 02.03)-Gloucester-Bristol (arr 04.26). One carriage taken from North Eastern TPO Up at Derby. Stock stabled at Bristol.

North Eastern Travelling Post Office Night Down
London, St Pancras (dep 22.23)-Derby (arr 00.11, dep 00.23)-Sheffield-York (arr 02.24, dep 02.31)-Darlington-Newcastle (arr 04.12). Takes one carriage from the Midland TPO at Derby. Stock stabled at Newcastle.

North Eastern Travelling Post Office Night Up
Newcastle (dep 20.22)-Darlington-York (arr 21.33, dep 22.14)-Sheffield-Derby (arr 00.12, dep 00.32)-Leicester-London, St Pancras (arr 03.00). Adds one carriage to the Midland TPO at Derby. Stock stabled at Cricklewood.

Top left:
Unloading from a York-built stowage van on the North Eastern TPO at Bedford on 26 September 1986. The decor is light blue and white.
Peter Johnson

Left:
No 47515 *Night Mail* at St Pancras preparing to remove the empty 'Flying Postman' stock to Cricklewood on 26 September 1986.
Peter Johnson

Above:
An interior view of sorting carriage No 80329 in use on the Whitehaven-Huddersfield TPO on 5 September 1985. This carriage was built at York in 1969 with a full set of exchange apparatus. *Peter Johnson*

Below:
Red-liveried postal stock at Kilby Bridge, Leicestershire, during the *Night Mail* filming runs on 20 September 1986. The locomotive is Class 47/4 No 47406 *Rail Riders*.
Peter Johnson

Right:
The 'Flying Postman' preparing to leave Bedford for St Pancras on 26 September 1986, powered by Class 47/4 No 47549 *Royal Mail*. *Peter Johnson*

THE FLYING POSTMAN

NORTH EAST'N T.P.O. NT. UP
25 SP
86
1
NORTH EAST'N T.P.O. NT. UP
25 SP
86
1
NORTH EAST'N T.P.O. NT. UP
25 SP
86
1
NORTH EAST'N T.P.O. NT. DOWN
24 SP
86
1
NORTH EAST'N T.P.O. NT. DOWN
24 SP
86
1
NORTH EAST'N T.P.O. NT. DOWN
24 SP
86
1
NORTH EASTERN T.P.O. NT. DOWN
26 SE
86
p.
MORE
TO
PAY
N.E.T.P.O.
26 SP
86
NIGHT DOWN

Top left:
The 'Flying Postmen'. Notice the new issue of grey smocks. *Peter Johnson*

Bottom left:
North Eastern TPO datestamps. The circular stamps on the bottom row are the reserves which were used on the 'Flying Postman'. A further six datestamps exist with the figure '2' at the bottom, as, presumably, do reserves for the Up TPO. *Peter Johnson*

Addenda to *The British Travelling Post Office*

I am grateful to Harold Wilson for passing to me a photocopy of a minute he found in the Post Office archives relating to the introduction of inter-vehicle gangways. Dated 7 May 1857 and addressed to the Postmaster General, it reads as follows:

1 The Midland Company having offered to establish a means of communication between the Travelling Post Office and the Tender which contains the Mail Bags so as to enable the Guard to pass from one to the other while the train is in motion, I instructed Mr Edward Page to accept the offer, and Your Grace will perceive that the proposal has now been carried into effect.

2 As this is the first instance in which the Department has obtained a means of communicating between the carriages, it is very satisfactory to find that the experiment has been successful, and in all probability great advantage will result from the facilities thus offered for obtaining greater space for sorting etc during the progress of the Train.

This minute predates the reference to the origin of gangways on page 41 of *The British Travelling Post Office* by two years.

Fred Sluter of the TPO Section kindly advised that the South Wales TPO operated between Neyland and Paddington for a period following World War 2. Beyond confirming that there was an 18.20 (SuO), 18.50 (SuX), Neyland departure, marked passenger and mail in the Winter 1961/62 Western Region working timetable, it has not yet been possible to establish the period of operation. Mr Sluter also pointed out that the photograph on page 89 of the above book actually shows the Midland TPO, not the York-Shrewsbury TPO which can just be seen behind.

That the Travelling Post Offices are only part of an integrated mail handling network is something that is not readily appreciated, so I was pleased to receive information relating to attempts to provide an improved service in the West Country before the war, when both road and air services were in their infancy. These observations came from W. K. Mackenzie, a retired Postal Controller, whose 1945 paper on TPOs includes a fascinating description of the work done by the Down Special.

An interesting account of the interlocking of the TPO network as observed at Bristol and Birmingham in 1978 is contained in a report of the Post Office Users National Council published in 1979. A member of the Council, Mr O. de Rousset-Hall, who was one of the observers, kindly provided a copy.

Reference was made to *The Traveller*, the defunct TPO staff magazine, although little was known about it. This attracted the attention of Dr Frank Scheer of the Railway Mail Service Library in Alexandria, Virginia, USA, who was able to track down and purchase an almost complete set of this rare publication, kindly sending a photocopy for examination. *The Traveller* was a printed monthly newsletter published by the TPO branch of the Union of Post Office Workers (now the Union of Communications Workers) from April 1946. It mainly contained items relating to working conditions and social events as well as some items of operational news. Publication ceased in October 1952 when subscriptions failed to cover printing costs of £11 per month.

Acknowledgements
My grateful thanks are extended to all those mentioned and especially to the gentlemen of the TPOs who have been so friendly, interested and co-operative — a special word here for Willie McCombe and Alex Obradovic of TPO Section. Also thanks to Jeremy Clarke, Tony Goodbody, Roger Harrison and Pete Roberts of the Railway Philatelic Group for providing information and mailing facilities, and to the Post Office Public Relations Officers who gave me the chance to participate in the events described.

Colourful Liveries for the 1980s: 1

Above:
The colourful appearance of two InterCity-liveried Class 86 electric locomotives is enhanced by the variously coloured containers in this Freightliner train approaching Stafford on 25 April 1986. *Chris Morrison*

Top right:
Undoubtedly the most eye-catching of the present crop of liveries is that developed for Network SouthEast. Class 50 No 50023 *Howe* was photographed at Salisbury with a four-coach train on 10 June 1986, the day when both the Network and its livery were launched. *G. F. Gillham*

Bottom right:
Although since returned to something much closer to its original green livery, Class 33 No 33008 *Eastleigh* nonetheless makes a fine sight in plain green with full yellow ends, approaching Waterloo with the Venice Simplon-Orient Express Pullmans returning from a Bournemouth excursion on 21 June 1986. *Chris Morrison*

Salisbury
3
50 023
Network SouthEast

MINERVA

Narrow Gauge Miscellany

The narrow gauge railways of North Wales are renowned for their variety and for the beauty of their surroundings. For one weekend in September 1986 the less scenic, but still highly interesting Leighton Buzzard Narrow Gauge Light Railway was able to offer the remarkable spectacle of nine working steam locomotives of eight different types. By way of contrast, both locations are featured; the Welsh lines as seen on 16-20 August 1986, and Leighton Buzzard on 21 September 1986.

All photographs by Peter Johnson

Far left:

Front-end contrasts at Page's Park. On the left, 0-4-0T Baguley (2007/1921) *Rishra* which spent its working life in India, and on the right, Kerr Stuart 'Wren' class 0-4-0ST (4256/1922) *Peter Pan*, which has no permanent base and travels to various functions from time to time. Page's Park is the main passenger terminus of the Leighton Buzzard Narrow Gauge Railway. *Peter Johnson*

Above left:

Stonehenge is the present terminus of the LBNGR and the site of the line's workshops. *Rishra* was photographed there with 1877-built 0-4-0VBT de Winton *Chaloner*. This distinctive vertical-boilered locomotive spent its working life at the Pen-yr-Orsedd Quarry in North Wales. *Peter Johnson*

Centre left:

Visitor *Wendy* is based on the private Hampshire Narrow Gauge Railway. A 0-4-0ST Bagnall product (2091/1919) it was supplied new to the Votty & Bowydd Slate Quarry at Blaenau Ffestiniog, later transferring to the Dorothea Quarry at Nantlle, Gwynedd. It is passing through the LBNGR's Leedon passing loop.
Peter Johnson

Below:

The LBNGR's own Kerr Stuart 'Wren' *Pixie* (4260/1922) stands at Page's Park with one of the railway's Simplex diesels on a demonstration freight.
Peter Johnson

Above:
Wood-burning Orenstein & Koppel 0-6-0WT *Elf* (12740/1936) approaches the Appenine Way level crossing bound for Page's Park, nearly 1½ miles away. This German-built locomotive spent its working life in the Cameroons.
Peter Johnson

Below:
Jurassic **was on loan from the Lincolnshire Coast Light Railway, which did not operate in 1986. This 0-6-0ST Peckett (1008/1903) spent its working life before preservation at the Southam Quarry in Warwickshire and is seen approaching Stonehenge Works.** *Peter Johnson*

Above:
The Festiniog's newest double Fairlie, *Earl of Merioneth* on the outskirts of Blaenau Ffestiniog, running alongside the Afon Barlwyd. *Peter Johnson.*

Below:
The Llanberis Lake Railway has two of the ubiquitous small Hunslet quarry locomotives in traffic, *Dolbadarn* (left) and *Elidir* (right), shown crossing at Cai Llydan, the half-way point of the railway. *Peter Johnson*

Top left:
The Llanberis Lake Railway's Gilfach Ddu terminus is adjacent to the North Wales Quarrying Museum which also owns a small Hunslet, *Una*. This locomotive is occasionally steamed during the summer when the driver is pleased to give footplate rides on the Museum's track. During 1986 it could also be seen on the LLR's Friday passenger service, substituting for one of the Lake Railway's own engines.
Peter Johnson

Centre left:
1986 was the first year of operation for the Fairbourne Railway in its 12¼in guise. The Mercedes diesel *Lilian Walter* is the only item of operating motive power to survive the change from 15in gauge. On the left is the Darjeeling 0-4-0ST *Sherpa*. *Peter Johnson*

Below:
The Festiniog Railway's *Mountaineer* is a much-travelled locomotive, being built in the US for service in France during World War 1 and seeing further service in France before being bought for preservation in the UK. In the autumn of 1986 it was travelling again, when it made a brief visit to the Vale of Rheidol Railway for an enthusiasts' weekend, being the first 'foreign' engine to work there since 1922. On that occasion the visitor was 0-4-0ST *Palmerston*, also from the FR. The location is Llanbadarn on 14 September 1985.
Norman Gurley

Far left:
Beyer Peacock 0-6-0T *The Countess* of the Welshpool & Llanfair Light Railway approaches New Drive crossing on the climb out of Welshpool (Raven Square). Withdrawn from use in 1969, the locomotive underwent an extensive overhaul before re-entering service in 1986. The inauguration of its return to traffic was undertaken by the Dowager Countess of Powis, who was on board the train with railway officials and guests.
Peter Johnson

Left:
During 1986 the Snowdon Mountain Railway introduced two Hunslet diesels of its own design, Nos 9 and 10. Intended for off-peak traffic and works trains, they are slightly shorter than the existing steam locomotives to allow them to work with planned longer coaches of higher capacity. No 10, now named *Yeti*, sets off up the mountain for the second time on a fine August day. No 9 has been named *Ninian*, after the Railway's Chairman.
Peter Johnson

Below:
Welsh Highland Railway 0-4-2T Peckett *Karen* is seen having been pressed into traffic on the mid-week service due to diesel failure. This locomotive worked for many years on an industrial railway in what was then Rhodesia (today known as Zimbabwe). *Peter Johnson*

Didcot Visitors

The Great Western Society celebrated its 25th anniversary in 1986. A visit to the Society's Didcot depot on 1 June of that year found several interesting visitors present.

All photographs by Hugh Ballantyne

Left:
'Dukedog' 4-4-0 No 3217 normally resides at the Bluebell Railway but underwent repair at Didcot. It is shown on the branch line with the goods train.

Below:
Making a briefer visit were LMS 'Jubilee' No 5690 *Leander* and Standard Class 4 No 75069, calling whilst on railtour duty from the Severn Valley Railway.

Left:
The most unusual sight was surely that of broad and standard gauge trains passing each other. The Science Museum's *Iron Duke* replica, loaned for the summer, is on the mixed-gauge Brunellian track whilst 2-6-2T No 5572 passes on the branch line.

Below left:
***Iron Duke* in the mixed-gauge transfer shed.**

Right:
Making its second visit to Didcot was '94XX' pannier tank No 9466 from the Buckinghamshire Steam Centre at Quainton. The GWR livery is strictly speaking spurious, for the locomotive was built by British Railways in 1952.

Colourful Liveries for the 1980s: 2

InterCity 125 power car No 43024 leads a HST set turned out in InterCity Sector livery passing Par on 2 July 1985.
John E. Oxley

Left:
A feature of the Sprinter DMUs is the attractive Provincial Sector livery, which is proving to be very photogenic. Working a Cambrian Coast 'Sunday Shuttle' on 17 August 1986, this set was photographed crossing the River Glaslyn between Porthmadog and Minffordd. In the far distance, above the right-hand car, can be seen the summit of Snowdon.
Peter Johnson

Below:
Two of the colour schemes carried by the New Generation diesel multiple-units are shown in this photograph of No 142071 (nearest) in Provincial Sector livery and No 144018 (beyond) in West Yorkshire PTE livery.
John E. Oxley

Two Veteran Austrian Electric Classes

Andrew Fox

A feature of various European railway networks is the survival in regular service of electric locomotives of a considerable age. In countries where electrification is widespread, the robust and relatively simple design of early electric locomotives often ensures them a prolonged life on less demanding duties after they have been displaced from the work for which they were originally built.

One country where this policy can be observed is Austria, where due to a combination of factors many of the earliest electric classes have attained working lives of 50 years or more. Although several of these became extinct in the late 1970s/early 1980s, others could at the time of writing still be seen in use on various parts of the Austrian Federal Railways (Österreichische Bundesbahnen). With the 150th anniversary of Austrian railways being celebrated in 1987, the following pages look at two of the most interesting designs to remain in service with the ÖBB in the anniversary year.

Class 1045

Type: Bo-Bo
Built: 1927-28
Weight: 61.2 tonnes
Axle load: 15.3 tonnes
Length over buffers: 10,300mm
Original number series: 1170.01-14
Electrical parts: ELIN
Mechanical parts: Wiener Neustadt (Nos 1170.01-10)
WLF Floridsdorf (Nos 1170.11-14)
Hourly rating: 1,140kW (at 40km/h)
Traction motors: 4
Wheel diameter: 1,300mm
Maximum speed: 60km/h

This class, of which 14 examples were built, was introduced in 1927 as Class 1170, principally for services on the secondary Salzkammergut line from Attnang-Puchheim to Stainach Irdning. On this difficult, winding route their maximum speed of 60km/h was not a particular handicap.

Right:
One of the last three surviving members of Class 1045. No 1045.009 shunts a trip freight working at Marchtrenk on the evening of 27 August 1986. This was one of the three regular diagrams for the class during the 1986 timetable. *Andrew Fox*

Although only built in limited numbers, and not intended for main line duties, the design represented a significant development in that it featured for the first time in Austria a Bo-Bo chassis with all axles individually powered, using Sécheron spring drive. In this system the traction motor is not mounted directly on the axle but on a hollow shaft, within which the axle is located. Power is transmitted by means of coil springs arranged around the wheel. These springs provide a flexible drive to convey tractive force to the wheel, and also absorb forces from the track. With the traction motor mounted directly on the bogie frames, unsprung masses can be kept to a minimum. In the case of Class 1045, buffers and couplings are mounted on the main superstructure of the locomotive, which carries all associated forces.

Improved versions of the design appeared in 1930 and 1934 (present-day Classes 1145 and 1245). In these classes, buffers and couplings are mounted on the bogies, obviating the need for the heavy frames which characterise Class 1045.

Members of the class continued to appear on local passenger services until the late 1970s, but were increasingly relegated to pick-up goods workings. Progressive withdrawal in recent years left only three examples in service at the start of 1986: Nos 1045.009/012/014, all based at their traditional home of Attnang-Puchheim depot. For these three locomotives there were three diagrams Monday-Friday in the 1986 working timetable. Despite deliveries of new electric locomotives to the ÖBB, the long-lived trio were all still in service on 1 January 1987.

Although the three ÖBB survivors were all scheduled for early withdrawal (which it was intended should take place during 1987), continued active service by the class was ensured on the private Montafonerbahn Bludenz-Schruns in the province of Vorarlberg at the western end of Austria. This electrified standard gauge railway purchased Nos 1045.01 and 1045.03 from the ÖBB in 1980. Within a short time No 1045.01 was given an overhaul and painted in the bright red and yellow livery of the MBS, whilst its companion had to wait until 1985 before being similarly treated. In addition the MBS acquired No 1045.06, withdrawn after minor accident damage, to serve as a source of spare parts.

Above:
This side view of No 1045.009 shows the very compact nature of the design, which resulted partly from a need to keep the locomotive's weight and hence axle loading as low as possible. Distinctive features include the heavy main frames carrying buffers and drawgear, and the equipment box in front of the No 2 end cab only. *Andrew Fox*

Below:
The final member of the class to remain in green livery was No 1045.012, seen stabled at Neumarkt-Kallheim station on 27 August 1986 between shunting duties. *Andrew Fox*

Above:
No 1045.014 is seen under repair at its home depot of Attnang-Puchheim on 29 August 1986. Both bogies have been removed for attention to the wheel sets and traction motors.
Andrew Fox

Left:
With various parts removed, including coupling rods and numbers, withdrawn Class 1080 locomotives Nos 1080.04 (nearest) and 1080.03 slumber in an overgrown siding at Selzthal depot on 3 September 1986. *Andrew Fox*

Below:
One of two red-liveried members of the class, No 1080.014 pilots a more modern Class 1042 Bo-Bo electric on a southbound freight at Traun, south of Linz, on 5 September 1986. *Andrew Fox*

Class 1080

Type: E
Built: 1924-25
Weight: 77 tonnes
Axle load: 15.4 tonnes
Length over buffers: 12,750mm
Original number series: 1080.01-20
Electrical parts: Siemens-Schuckert, Wien
Mechanical parts: Krauss & Co, Linz
Hourly rating: 990kW (at 38km/h)
Traction motors: 3
Wheel diameter: 1,350mm
Maximum speed: 50km/h

Built to a total of 20 examples, Class 1080 was introduced in 1924 as the first Austrian electric freight locomotive. The three centre axles are powered by one traction motor each, and all 10 wheels of this rigid frame design are coupled by conventional steam locomotive-style coupling rods. Thus, although the two outer axles have no traction motors, the entire weight of the locomotive can be utilised for adhesion. The obvious disadvantage is that the chassis is relatively inflexible and is not particularly suited to routes with sharp curvature.

Just as improved versions of Class 1045 were built, similarly Class 1080 was developed in the form of Classes 1180 and 1280, which appeared in 1926 and 1927 respectively.

With their very restrictive maximum speed of only 50km/h, the members of Class 1080 were relegated to secondary duties as more modern designs became available. In the 1950s they were modified for trip freight working and heavy shunting at larger yards, which have been their main spheres of operation during recent years.

At the start of 1987 only half of the class remained in service, allocated to Attnang-Puchheim and Selzthal depots, but sometimes travelling some distance from these two places in the course of their work.

Despite their antiquity and the fact that these two classes are currently being withdrawn, they were both included in the ÖBB's new computerised numbering scheme. This adds a zero digit before the individual locomotive number, as well as adding a final computer check digit. Thus, for example, No 1080.01 becomes No 1080.001-9.

Below:
On a misty 15 July 1985, the first member of Class 1080 was on pilot duties at Stainach Irdning, the junction station at the southern end of the Salzkammergut line from Attnang-Puchheim. At this date the locomotive still carried its original number as 1080.01. *Andrew Fox*

Top left:
Proudly displaying its computerised identity, No 1080.011 awaits it next duty at Nettingsdorf, south of Linz, on 29 August 1986. *Andrew Fox*

Centre left:
The end of the line for No 1045.07 at Attnang-Puchheim on 15 July 1985. In the background withdrawn No 1080.09 awaits the same fate. This unusual view shows well the principal features of the Class 1045 design, particularly the Sécheron spring drive which is clearly visible on the axle unit in the foreground. *Andrew Fox*

Below:
The Montafonerbahn between Bludenz and Schruns in the far West of Austria should offer the chance to see Class 1045 at work long after the withdrawal of the last ÖBB examples. On 27 July 1985 No 1045.01, dating from 1927, stands in the yard opposite the ÖBB station at Bludenz at the head of a train of stone hoppers. Alongside is ÖBB No 1180.003, of a design closely related to Class 1080.
Andrew Fox

Above:
A popular attraction whenever it appears in public is the Stirling Single 4-2-2 No 1, which aroused great interest on the occasion of its visit to the Great Central Railway in 1981. It appeared in steam regularly and is seen leaving Loughborough in May 1982. *Peter Johnson*

Below:
The Rutland Railway Museum is based on part of a former ironstone railway between the villages of Cottesmore and Ashwell. Brake van rides and demonstration freight trains are run using both steam and diesel locomotives. Hawthorn Leslie 0-4-0ST (3856/1936) *Singapore* returns to the depot with a goods train on 28 September 1986. The locomotive was supplied new to HM Dockyard in Singapore, was captured by the Japanese during the war, and returned to the UK in 1953. *Peter Johnson*

Leicestershire Steam

Less well known than the GCR is the Market Bosworth Light Railway, whose 0-6-0ST Bagnall (2670/1942) *Lamport No 3* is seen en route for Market Bosworth on 6 May 1985. The railway has plans to extend to Shenton, location of the Bosworth battlefield visitors' centre. *Peter Johnson*

Britomart

Tony Massau

On one of the best-known narrow gauge railways in the British Isles there can be found one of the not so well-known preserved locomotives, the 0-4-0 saddle tank *Britomart*, built by Hunslet in 1899, works No 707. This locomotive is typical of the many small Hunslets once to be found in the Welsh slate quarries, and spent her working life at Pen-yr-Orsedd slate quarry, Nantlle, Caernarvonshire. By the early 1960s many of these hard-working engines were idle as the quarries either went out of business altogether or adopted alternative transportation methods.

Getting settled round a table in the 'Ship and Castle' at Portmadoc one winter's evening in early 1965 with Festiniog Railway colleagues Bob Harris and Roger Goss, I was suddenly confronted with the offer to join them in forming a small group to attempt the purchase of one of these quarry locomotives before the price increased dramatically as was threatened. Possibly I was the only person they could think of who might have some spare cash, as preserved railway employees were not exactly overpaid in those days. In due course, Steve Coulson and the late Tom Baskcomb, both regular Boston Lodge works volunteers of long standing, joined the group. Our attentions settled on the Pen-yr-Orsedd quarry at Nantlle and we joined forces with Tony Hills, who also has a story to tell about this transaction, to make a joint purchase of the Hunslet 0-4-0ST sisters *Britomart* and *Una*, at what, even in 1965 could have been said to be a modest price.

The engines had been out of service for a while and stored in a shed on the first level of the quarry above ground. This caused some problems to the hired low-loader in negotiating

Left:
Roger Goss shunting *Britomart* with World War 1 Simplex *Mary Ann* at Boston Lodge Works on 17 May 1966. *A. N. Massau*

Above:
***Britomart* being shunted at Boston Lodge before the overhaul commenced. Notice the dumb buffers and chain link coupling. The cab components are in the bogie wagon.**
Paul Ingham collection

Right:
An owners' special on 8 April 1967. *Britomart* pauses at Cae Mawr whilst Roger Goss and Tom Baskcomb check the engine over. *A. N. Massau*

Britomart and former Pen-yr-Orsedd colleague *Chaloner* were the stars of the Festiniog Railway 150 celebration on 19/20 April 1986. Standing on the mineral line at Minffordd, they wait to haul their train of slate wagons up to Gwindy, where the wagons will be released to run back by gravity. *Peter Treloar*

the rough and twisting track up to the locomotive shed. The two locomotives were winched aboard and an even more perilous descent began with the trailer having to be skidded around at least one hairpin bend against a packing wall of sleepers and then careering out of control down the final hill to ground level. Fortunately the driver regained command of his vehicle without incident upon reaching the level approach to the main road, and a somewhat calmer journey ensued to Portmadoc Harbour station. Here *Britomart* was unloaded on to the Welsh Highland spur outside the goods shed and said farewell to sister *Una* who continued on to pastures new.

Britomart was towed across the Cob by the diesel *Moelwyn* and into Boston Lodge works, where during the weeks leading up to the purchase we had constructed a small shed in the top yard and relaid the approach trackwork to it. To gain access to the shed involves the use of one of the wagon turntables surviving from the pre-preservation yard layout. As *Britomart* is privately owned and only on the Festiniog Railway by the kind hospitality of the management, the owners place some importance on not allowing the locomotive to get in the way or become a nuisance in the works, hence the construction of its own exclusive shed in a quiet part of the Boston Lodge complex.

With the locomotive now in our hands, an overhaul soon commenced, with work taking place several evenings in the week and some weekends. Compared to the work facing the owners of engines rescued from Barry in recent years, ours was indeed a simple task, being little more than a routine overhaul of a serviceable locomotive. The main items of renewal were the boiler tubes and the smokebox. One new piece of equipment was fitted. This was an ejector placed under the footplating; the object being to draw water out of a convenient line-side stream with hosepipe attachments, and project it into the saddle tank. *Britomart* had much less water capacity than the Festiniog engines and in those days one could only take on water at Portmadoc, Boston Lodge and Tan-y-Bwlch.

Britomart was lit up for the first time by the late Bill Hoole on the afternoon of 5 July 1966, the location being the old locomotive shed now used for winter carriage storage. She was still without the cab and was only painted in undercoat. Steam was raised by evening and a small gathering of staff and volunteers gathered to witness the first movements on the shed approach roads and subsequently try their hands at the regulator. The evening was judged a success and spurred us on to completion of the rebuild. Just over one month passed to find me photographing the engine at the same location, complete with cab and resplendent in Great Northern Railway of Ireland blue with maroon frames. She ran a trial trip to Minffordd with a couple of wagons on 20 August, and the following evening ran again to the same station with a celebration special comprising the buffet and observation coaches of the old stock. The engine performed well, the main problem area being the lifting injectors fitted on the firebox backhead which proved difficult to start once the water level in the saddle tank became low. The old trick of pouring cold water over the injectors to cool them down prevented the problem from getting out of hand.

The next significant step forward came on 8 April 1967 when *Britomart* set out for Tan-y-Bwlch with a bogie wagon and No 1 brake van loaded with various pioneering guests. The water-lifting ejector proved its worth by replenishing the saddle tank from the stream at Gysgfa curves, about a mile into the wooded section between Penrhyn and Tan-y-Bwlch. There is no doubt that the fitting of this small additional piece of equipment vindicated itself, for it would have been impossible to complete the journey to Tan-y-Bwlch without taking on water by some means. Gysgfa became the regular water stop on all subsequent *Britomart* trips, some of which have included haulage of the buffet and observation coaches used on our first runs to Minffordd, already mentioned.

Tan-y-Bwlch was reached without incident although naturally at a more pedestrian pace than with the Festiniog's own engines. Whilst this was just the forerunner of several such trips over the years, *Britomart* has, by token of our appreciation to the company, performed useful tasks for the railway in her accustomed role of shunter and short-haul trip working. Coal empties from Boston Lodge to Minffordd have been handled, returning with loaded wagons. She has also proved capable of shunting six coach rakes of carriages around Harbour station with ease.

In August 1972 *Britomart* was a major attraction in the annual Portmadoc Carnival. She was mounted on the trailer of the FR Co's articulated lorry, in steam, on special rollers so that the wheels and motion could rotate whilst the lorry toured the crowded streets. One of the original FR four-wheeled coaches was also on the lorry's trailer, coupled to *Britomart*. The coach contained various FR personalities in period costume. The following year *Britomart* was used in another public relations exercise, this time as a static exhibit at the Transpo 73 Exhibition in Manchester.

Since the changeover to oil-firing of the Festiniog's own fleet in the early 1970s, *Britomart* has had the distinction of being the only coal-burning locomotive to operate on the line although she is not allowed further than Tan-y-Bwlch because of the fire risk to Forestry plantations.

In more recent times steam power has been fitted to the engine's own brakes, and vacuum equipment to operate train brakes. This is to comply with safety regulations, necessary even for small private parties in one coach and will make the engine even more useful on such duties as carriage inspection and maintenance shunting and other duties involving vacuum-braked stock. Lately the locomotive has run specials in connection with FR courses held at the Snowdonia National Park Study Centre, Plas Tan-y-Bwlch and it played a special part in the 1986 FR150 celebrations, too. Proposed for 1987 is the operation of *Britomart*-hauled trains to Rhiw Goch loop. It has been suggested that *Britomart* might make an interesting engine to employ on the Dinas branch shuttle trains in Blaenau Ffestiniog if this prospect eventually becomes reality. However, that is something to speculate on for the future.

Above left:
Taking water at Gysgfa.
A. N. Massau

Left:
Tan-y-Bwlch is reached for the first time. *A. N. Massau*

Above:
With saddle tank and cab removed, *Britomart* sits up on blocks in the Boston Lodge erecting shop whilst undergoing boiler repairs on 9 March 1986. *Peter Johnson*

Centre right:
Preparing for FR150 — on 18 April 1986 *Britomart* was used to shunt Boston Lodge yard. Driver Paul Ingham found it easier to attend to the fire whilst the locomotive was stationary between moves.
Peter Johnson

Bottom right:
In September 1986 *Britomart* travelled to Bedfordshire and earned herself a starring role on the Leighton Buzzard Light Railway during a stay which covered three weekends. 20/21 September was the enthusiasts' weekend and *Britomart* was photographed at Page's Park during Sunday morning shunting operations.
Peter Johnson

Merseyside Electrics

The Merseyrail suburban system continues to maintain its vitality, despite mass unemployment in the areas which it serves. On 30 September 1985 electrification was extended further into the Wirral, from Rock Ferry to Hooton, in a scheme costing £5 million. On 6 April of the following year, the centenary of the former Mersey Railway was celebrated in fine style.

All photographs by Mike Haddon

Above:
The last of the LMS 1938 electric multiple-units (BR Class 503) was restored to its original livery and used to convey dignitaries from Rock Ferry to Hooton on 30 September 1985.

Top right:
On arrival at Hooton it was possible to contrast the 1938 set with the modern Class 508 unit operating the public service.

Bottom right:
A more typical scene, at Bebington, on the first day of the electric service, with Class 508 unit No 508116.

Hooton
ROCK FERRY TO HOOTON
ELECTRIFICATION
LMS
Liverpool
508 110

Hooton
508 116

Liverpool
508 117
Merseyrail

Left:
Two Class 508 sets at Rock Ferry with a through service to Liverpool. Prior to electrification the service was operated by Modernisation Plan DMUs which terminated at Rock Ferry.

Above:
In celebrating the Mersey Railway centenary, events focused on Birkenhead with preserved stock operating services as far as Hoylake on the West Kirby line. The preserved LMS Southport line Class 502 driving cars are shown at Hoylake.

Below:
Although owned by the National Railway Museum, this unit is kept at Steamport, Southport, where it was restored.

Private
RIBBLE
CK 3825

GAWSWORTH HALL
GAWSWORTH HALL
GAWSWORTH HALL
GAWSWORTH HALL
L.G.O.C.
SERVICE 58
HAMMERSMITH
TG&LB
RCUS

Top left:
The restored Ribble 1927 Leyland Lion loading passengers near Rock Ferry station before making a run to Port Sunlight, a route once operated by Mersey Railway buses.

Bottom left:
An even older form of road transport was used to carry visitors to the Shore Road pumping station. The London-liveried horse bus was photographed outside Hamilton Square station. Access to the pumping station was limited, so overcrowding was eliminated by admitting only those who travelled on the horse bus.

Right:
The public was admitted to Birkenhead North depot, where they were able to see the heavy repair shop crane lift an EMU car as part of a bogie removal demonstration.

Below:
Other rolling stock displayed included a Sprinter Class 150/1 DMU and former Midland line DMU power cars converted and given a green livery for parcels use.

The Dieppe Route to Paris

C. R. L. Coles

Of the recognised rail routes linking London with Paris, that via Dieppe is the most direct — the overall distance between the two capitals being approximately 41 miles less than via the short sea route.

It was in 1847 that the first continental service across the English Channel from Newhaven to Dieppe was inaugurated by what was then known as the Brighton & Continental Steam Packet Co. However, because of strong objections from the South Eastern Railway the project encountered legal problems and the service was transferred to a concern with the name Maples & Morris, which commenced operations between these two ports in 1851. By 1862 these matters had been sorted out when a joint service between the LB&SCR and the Western Railway of France (Chemin de fer de l'Ouest) became established — Maples & Morris continuing to operate on behalf of the two railway companies until 1867 by which time the LB&SCR had acquired a fleet of paddle steamers which could cover the distance in 4hr 20min.

Below:
Ex-SECR Class F 4-4-0 No 1443 piloting an unidentified 'H2' class 4-4-2 passing Clapham Junction in 1939 with a Victoria-Newhaven boat train. *C. R. L. Coles*

Apart from interruptions during the two war periods in the present century, this service has continued ever since and today the continental timetable lists a minimum of two journeys daily (except on Christmas Day and Boxing Day) each way throughout the year with additional sailings during busy periods according to the volume of traffic.

To the railway enthusiast, parts of the route (mainly between London and Newhaven) are already very familiar and have been thoroughly documented, both in text and photographically, within the realms of railway literature. I have therefore decided that the pictures chosen for this article, aided by their respective captions, shall themselves tell this side of the story and, in the text, to concentrate more on the environmental and historical features. Little attention need be given to the first few miles through London's suburbs until we are heading towards the line of the North Downs ahead. Here, as we follow a rising gradient of 1 in 264 through a deep chalk cutting towards Quarry Tunnel, we see a marked change in the immediate surroundings which vary according to season. Where railway cuttings offer almost complete protection to wildlife, we may, in springtime, see an abundance of primroses which seem to thrive on chalky soil whereas in summer we may well find one or more species of scabious adding colour to the scene. But it is when approaching the Sussex Weald towards Three Bridges that we meet up with what is, beyond doubt, the greatest change in the face of the environment since World War 2. What, at that time, was a racecourse has been completely transformed, and incorporated in London's second air terminal. The former Gatwick Racecourse station has been completely rebuilt and renamed Gatwick Airport to cater for the greatly increased volume of passenger traffic whilst the original Gatwick Airport station, approximately one mile further south, no longer exists. We may also see one or more of the 'Gatwick Express' trains in their distinctive livery which now provide a fast and frequent service between Gatwick and Victoria station. But this is not all. The importance of Gatwick Airport is such that even the advertised boat trains to and from Newhaven now call here as well as at East Croydon.

Continuing on the Brighton line, the boat trains branch left at Keymer Junction towards Lewes where the line from Brighton (via Falmer) comes in on our right. At one time two other lines also converged on Lewes: from East Grinstead and from Tunbridge Wells. Neither exist today in their entirety as through routes. Although very little of the town can be seen from the train as we pass through the station, Lewes, which lies in the gap where the River Ouse flows through the South Downs, is a most attractive place containing many fine buildings of historical and cultural interest, some dating back to the

Left:
A Newhaven boat train leaving Victoria station's platform 15 headed by electric locomotive No 20003 circa 1950. This service is now operated by main line electric multiple-unit stock, the trains being worked to/from the eastern side of the terminus. *British Rail*

Left:
Captain Beale, Master of BR's SS *Londres*, photographed on the bridge of his ship as it neared Dieppe in May 1959. *C. R. L. Coles*

Below:
Sealink MV *Senlac* of 5,590 tons, photographed at Newhaven in November 1978. *Les Bertram*

Bottom:
The SS *Arromanches* was built in 1946 and withdrawn from service in 1965, after which she served for a further five years in Greek waters. She was photographed alongside SNCF Class 231D Pacific No 231D685 at Dieppe Maritime in May 1964.
Brian Haresnape

Right:
A former Etat 4-6-2, photographed at Dieppe from the deck of a cross-channel ferry circa 1934.
C. R. L. Coles collection

11th century, and is well worth a visit. From here the railway continues through the valley of the Ouse to Southerham Junction (where the Eastbourne line branches to the left) then over the concluding 5½ miles to Newhaven Harbour. Though spoiled by modern building, Newhaven has much to recall early days when it was known as Meeching. The Ouse at one time flowed parallel to the Sussex coast to reach the sea at Seaford — a small seaside resort with a shingle beach some four to five miles further east. But over the centuries the river mouth became gradually shifted by this eastern drift of shingle until during a violent storm in 1578, the much swollen river burst its banks to meet the sea at what is now the present harbour — which then became known as 'New Haven'.

A strong south-westerly wind greeted us when we boarded the 2,404-ton British Railways SS *Londres* for the four-hour crossing to Dieppe. With a moderate swell in the English Channel we could therefore expect the ship to roll and pitch. At that time this vessel had already seen 19 years' service so it could well be that she was approaching the end of her career as a cross-channel ferry. With the waves crashing over her bows, more especially as we approached the French coast, I wanted, if possible, to capture this scene with my movie camera. Accordingly I wormed my way to the bridge where a word with Captain Beale did the trick!

With a population of over 26,000 inhabitants, Dieppe, besides being a channel port, is the oldest seaside resort in France and the nearest to Paris. It dates back to the 14th century. Dieppe and other places in the vicinity were the primary objective of a

reconnaissance raid in August 1942 when, under the codename 'Operation Jubilee' a force of about 7,000 commandos, mostly Canadian, took part. Although more than 5,000 men were lost in this operation, essential information was obtained and put to good use in the preparations for D-Day in June 1944.

Two routes link Dieppe with Paris: via Rouen and the Seine Valley, or via Gisors. The principal boat trains take the former route, calling at Rouen in both directions. This then affords us an opportunity of spending a while in this most interesting city. With a population of nearly 320,000 inhabitants, Rouen is one of France's main river ports and the capital of Upper Normandy. Its principal tourist attraction is the Notre Dame cathedral which dates back to the 12th century. It was also in Rouen that Joan of Arc spent her last days before being burned at the stake on 30 May 1431. The tower, which is the former keep in Phillipe Auguste's castle where she was imprisoned, is open to the public and here a number of mementoes concerning Joan of Arc and her fate are on display. The oldest part of the city contains many half-timbered houses situated on the right bank of the Seine. Much of this area was destroyed during World War 2 but has since been completely restored. The cathedral also suffered heavily and is still in the process of restoration. Henry II, the first of the Plantagenet kings, lies buried here as also is the heart of his son, Richard the Lionheart, who succeeded to the English throne to become Richard I following the death of his father in 1189.

One of the prime objectives of the allied forces during the months preceding D-Day in June 1944 was to paralyse the entire railway system throughout Normandy, thus disrupting the enemy lines of communication. Mantes-la-Jolie, some 35 miles west of Paris (and where most long-distance trains call), was one of many towns and villages which suffered considerable devastation both before and after the D-Day landings which took place some 70-odd miles west of the route over which we are now travelling. Yet in 1959, as we made our first journey through Normandy to Paris, it was difficult to believe that only 15 years had elapsed since the German 7th Army were forced to surrender in August 1944. We saw no outward signs of war damage; railways, towns and villages had all been rebuilt or restored. Mantes-la-Jolie is an attractive town with English connections in that, in September 1087, William the Conqueror sustained fatal injuries when his horse trod on a burning cinder whilst the town was on fire and causing the king to fall heavily. By that time he had welded into one unit first the Duchy of Normandy and then the Kingdom of England to such an extent that free trade became established between the ports of Normandy and both Southampton and London. Fortunately, the 12th century church of Notre Dame escaped war damage as also did the nearby Château de Rosny which contains numerous works of art and tapestries for which this part of France can justly claim to be famous. Mantes-la-Jolie continues its Anglo-French connections in that it is now 'twinned' with the London Borough of Hillingdon with whom a number of exchange visits have been made in recent years.

I have deliberately been digressing somewhat because Normandy has borne witness to

Left:
An express from Le Havre, headed by Class 231D 4-6-2 No 231D695 approaching the Gare St Lazare, Paris, in May 1959. Beyond the signalbox on the left is a train of double-deck coaches, whilst in the short spur between these and the express is Class 231G 4-6-2 No 231G516 awaiting its next turn of duty. An electric suburban train approaches the tunnel on the left. *C. R. L. Coles*

Right:
A general view of the Gare St Lazare showing '141TD' 2-8-2T No 141TD101 leaving the terminus with a local train. Electric suburban trains which collect current from an outside third rail use the tracks on the extreme right of this picture. *C. R. L. Coles*

a series of events which, had they gone the other way, might well have completely altered history. Back now to the main line from Le Havre to Paris which we joined at Rouen. From here to Paris the railway follows the valley of the Seine which is mainly a tourist area on account of its natural beauty and many castles built upon the river banks. The river is said to derive its present name from the Latin *sequana* and from the Celtic *squan* meaning to curve or bend — its many U-turns flowing first one way and then the other through mainly rural country studded with pasture land, orchards, farms and other smallholdings. Gradients are mainly slight and generally in favour of westbound traffic and there are several level stretches; indeed it is interesting to record that, at one time during the steam age, water troughs were installed on this particular main line.

In 1959 the main lines west of Paris over what was formerly the Etat system (now the Western Region of the SNCF) were still steam operated and, on the Dieppe, Le Havre and Rouen lines a varied assortment of four-cylinder de Glehn compound 4-6-2s monopolised long-distance passenger services. Dating back to 1914 when the first of these engines had been developed by the Etat, they became known as the 231.500 series and, in subsequent years up to 1923, the French Ministry of Public Works placed orders for no fewer than 400 locomotives of this type — to be built by various firms and of which 45 were constructed by the North British Locomotive Co in Glasgow. Of these 400 engines, 280 went to the Etat, the remainder being allocated to other French railways.

Most of the Etat engines were rebuilt during 1933-37 embodying Chapelon principles but with detail differences — mainly relating to valve gear and exhaust. As rebuilt, they were reclassified types 'D', 'F', 'G' and 'H' — the '231Gs' being the most powerful. Short-distance suburban passenger trains were worked by 2-8-2 tank locomotives, series 'TC' and 'TD', whilst the '141R' class American-built 2-8-2s (of which an example is preserved at Bressingham) could be seen on freight trains.

No less attractive, especially during springtime when the many orchards in this part of Normandy provide a blaze of colour, is the less familiar alternative route via Gisors and over which relief boat trains are sometimes booked. This line follows the valley of the smaller River Epte and serves a number of small towns of which Neufchatel-en-Bray and Gournay-en-Bray are centres

from which local dairies supply the major part of fresh cheese consumed in France. This line continues through mainly pastoral country to Pontoise and Enghien where it joins the Seine valley line from Rouen. Now the first sign of our approaching Paris comes into view — ahead to our left we see the basilica of Sacré Coeur crowning the hill of Montmartre; a landmark for many miles around Paris.

Paris has been described as the most charming city in the world — a city that never goes to sleep. We knew what we were going to see on this, our first visit — it had already been planned. We also knew what we hoped to see during our 10-day stay, and that there would be much that we would not be able to see for want of time. But to be able to find such an opportune vantage point as the Place de l'Europe from which excellent railway pictures could be obtained was something which we did not expect — until we had studied a street map of the city. Being also within a short walking distance from our hotel, I was able to spend the odd hour or two here during which several pictures around Gare St Lazare were taken without upsetting our other prearranged plans. But perhaps our most thrilling impression of Paris, which I recorded on movie film, was from the top of the 984ft-high Eiffel Tower under perfect visibility. It is said that the top of the tower can sway to and fro by as much as 6ft according to weather conditions. We certainly did not notice any such movement despite the fact that the whole structure is supported on compressed air.

Our most recent journey through Normandy was by the late night boat train hauled by a series '86000' class diesel-electric locomotive and which was timed to leave the Gare St Lazare at 22.30. Earlier that day we had travelled back from the Rhône Valley reaching Paris late in the afternoon. This final journey to Dieppe was, compared with the run from Valence, somewhat of an anti-climax. Darkness had set in, little could be seen from the carriage windows and there were no refreshments to be had on this train. A few hours hence and the chalk outline of the Seven Sisters along the Sussex coast would be spelling 'Welcome Home' to us at the end of another holiday. But for the moment we were still in France. Then, as if by magic, as we approached Rouen, there stood out bathed in floodlight like a beacon against the night sky, the cathedral of Notre Dame; its tall slender iron spire pointing to the heavens and proclaiming the Christian message to all. A perfect ending to a perfect holiday.

Industrial Grime

A regular feature in *Railway World* is entitled 'Industrial Pride'. Here Tom Heavyside presents his view of the latter years of the British industrial steam scene.

All photographs by Tom Heavyside

Left:
A frosty morning at Fryston colliery as Hunslet 'Austerity' 0-6-0ST No 3168/1944 sets off back to Wheldale colliery with a mixture of empty NCB internal user wagons on 10 December 1981.

Above:
The sites of many industrial railways were rarely suitable for either locomotives or men and conditions scarcely rose above the basic. A Bagnall 'Austerity' 0-6-0ST (2758/1944) stands outside the basic shed facility at Pontardulais (northwest of Swansea) on 20 September 1979. The shed formerly served Graig Merthyr colliery, closed by this time, and the locomotive was now used to shunt wagons at the nearby blending site.

Above right:
Nearing the end of a shift; with work-stained clothing and features the driver of No 2758 looks happy coaling up on 24 May 1973. Now you can see why the locomotive stands outside the shed!

Right:
Sometimes the railways came closer to residential areas than was conducive to keeping a clean environment, but even then the pedestrians appear able to ignore the passing of two smoke-emitting monsters and their train. Ex-GWR 0-6-0PT No 7754 (now undergoing restoration on the Llangollen Railway) and Avonside 0-6-0ST (1680/1914) *Sir John* bank a diesel-hauled train away from Mountain Ash. It was bound for Aberaman Phurnacite Plant at Abercwmboi on 5 October 1971. This section of track once formed part of the GWR Pontypool-Neath line

Left:
Even taking a distant view does not separate the houses from the spoil tips. At the head of Rhondda Fach Valley on 8 October 1971 Peckett 0-6-0ST 2150/1954 moves empty wagons out of the BR exchange sidings for Maerdy colliery, part of which can be seen behind the sidings.

Top:
Robert Stephenson & Hawthorn 'Austerity' 0-6-0ST No 8 (7139/1944), rebuilt by Hunslet in 1961 as their No 3880, shunts coal over the weighbridge at Mountain Ash on 21 September 1979.

Above:
On a gloomy 28 March 1974 at Savile colliery, Hunslet No S111 (1956/1939) shunts a train of internal user wagons.

29
NCB

Top left:
The acrid smell of a coking plant adds a further dimension to the proceedings as Hawthorn Leslie 0-6-0ST Coal Products No 3 (3575/1923) shunts the Glasshoughton Coking Plant at Castleford, Yorkshire, on 21 August 1974.

Bottom left:
With a backdrop of the colliery slag heap, Hawthorn Leslie 0-4-0ST No 3072/1914 *Shakespeare* waits for time at Bersham colliery, Rhostyllen, near Wrexham, on 21 August 1973.

Above:
A council housing estate forms a contrasting backdrop at Haig colliery, Whitehaven, on 30 August 1974 as Giesl-fitted Hunslet 'Austerity' No 3698/1950 *Repulse* does the work.

NCB
St DUNSTAN

Top left:
Even in Kent, the garden of England, industrial grime was to be found at Snowdown colliery. On 16 September 1974 Avonside 0-6-0ST *St Dunstan* (2004/1927) was at work. The engine was named for the 25th Archbishop of Canterbury.

Bottom left:
***C'est magnifique, mais ce n'est pas le clean air.* Double-headed Barclays No 8 (1175/1909) leading No 25 (2358/1954) approach the BR exchange sidings on Polkemmet Moor in pouring rain on 23 May 1974. No 8 is now mounted on a plinth at the Polkemmet colliery entrance.**

Right:
Despite the conditions, driver James Spiers always did his best to overcome the industrial grime found at Kinneil colliery and kept Barclay 0-4-0ST NCB No 21 (2292/1951) looking immaculate. He was captured throwing out the fire on 23 May 1974.

Below:
Barclay 0-4-0ST No 1614/1918 blows off whilst waiting for the rubbish wagons to be emptied on one of the Waterside system's tips on 29 August 1973. A more typically desolate industrial scene could hardly be imagined.

London: World Steam Centre

A. E. Durrant

Ask the average British enthusiast where was the largest steam centre of all time, and names like Crewe, Newcastle and Glasgow will proliferate. Americans will probably go for Chicago, Australians will opt for the capital city of whichever state they reside in, and the rest of the world will exhibit various degrees of bewilderment. Few would think of London, capital city of the world's greatest empire, achieving greatness largely during the Victorian era, when steam railways were the world's last great civilising influence, bringing order out of the chaos of darkest Africa, inscrutable Asia, and the frontiers of the Americas. But, enough of resounding clichés, and down to some facts and figures.

The Southern

The greatest steam show of all must have been London before electrification started south of the Thames, but even the author, relatively ancient as he is in today's youthful society, cannot claim familiarity with that scene. Although born and bred in the then mainly electrified area south of the Thames, the author got to know London during the wartime 1940s, and his first individual 'bash' was a Sunday afternoon jaunt from Sunbury-on-Thames to Clapham Junction in the winter of, perhaps, 1942. Imagine a remarkably naïve and ignorant schoolboy, investing the pennies of his pocket money

Above:
Typical of the author's first wartime Clapham Junction 'bash' was a 'King Arthur' rolling through on a Waterloo-bound passenger working. In this case No 30453 *King Arthur* is probably on a boat train, certainly not part of the wartime scene! *A. E. Durrant*

Left:
The Southern had arguably the most handsome tank engines in Britain and the 'W' class three-cylinder 2-6-4T were perhaps the best looking of all. No 31921 is seen near Scrubs Lane on a typical transfer trip from Old Oak Common to the Southern. *A. E. Durrant*

Below left:
Competing for massive good looks with the 'W' class were the LSWR's 'H16' class 4-6-2T. No 30517 crosses the Thames at Barnes Bridge with a mixed freight bound for its home depot of Feltham. *A. E. Durrant*

into an afternoon trip which was more a journey into the unknown than subsequent visits to the far corners of the earth. There was 0-8-0T No 949 *Hecate* loose shunting passenger carriages as though they were goods wagons, in company with 'M7' and 'O2' 0-4-4Ts, although I am not sure that these classifications were known to me at the time. The main line had steam passenger services (mainly 'King Arthurs') at roughly hourly intervals each way, and on the Brighton side were several passenger trains, steam hauled, by 4-4-2Ts. Being wartime, there were some Sunday freights and I remember an LMS 0-6-0 (a '4F'?), and just before returning to Sunbury, an incredible machine which emerged from the misty murk, an LNER 0-6-2T with huge pipes each side of the smokebox, and a hoarse, asthmatic, exhaust beat. This, of course, was later identified as an 'N1'.

Having returned unscathed from this great Clapham Junction safari, my parents were soon convinced that all-day trips into London were devoid of likely hazard, and with the odd schoolboy companion, I commenced Saturday trips, up to Waterloo by Southern, and then by Underground to the numerous termini spread across London; these developed later into adventurous sorties along the suburban routes to likely-looking junctions or centres where more locomotives could be seen. It must be remembered that at this time there were no Ian Allan *abcs*, and for the beginner, due to the wartime clampdown on magazines, the discovery of a new and rare type of locomotive was as exciting and common as it was in Indonesia in the 1970s!

For the novice, the Southern, even though largely electrified, had a huge and varied collection of steam power, for main line passenger services, outer suburban trains, and all freight, shunting, and empty stock movements. Steam passenger trains started and terminated at Waterloo, Charing Cross, Victoria, Cannon Street, London Bridge (low level), and Holborn Viaduct. There were central steam locomotive depots at Nine Elms, Stewarts Lane, Bricklayers Arms, and New Cross Gate, while slightly further out there were Feltham, Hither Green and Norwood Junction sheds, serving mainly freight and shunting duties, each with its own exotic locomotive class rarely seen elsewhere — the 'G16' 4-8-0T at Feltham, 'Z' class 0-8-0T at Hither Green, and the 'E6X' large-boilered 0-6-2T at Norwood.

Although some 20 years had passed since grouping, the older locomotives remained very much on their original home grounds, and some of the more restricted denizens, mainly tank engines, were very difficult to see at all, as wartime conditions meant no permitted visits to sheds. Many were the long explorations through side streets, seeking for vantage points overlooking shed yards, to see such exotica as crane tank No 1302 at Stewarts Lane, plus the old 'T' class Nos 1602 and 1604 at the same depot. Bricklayers Arms housed the sole 'S' class, No 1685, also very difficult to see. All four main lines had locomotives designed and built especially for the London area, and the Southern had more such specialities than the others. It was a very different Southern than was familiar in the 1960s, when Bulleid Pacifics were so prolific. In the wartime years of the early 1940s the handful of 'Merchant Navy' class were comparative rarities, and one was more likely to see a Drummond 'Paddlebox'!

To quantify the above, the Southern, in the mid-1940s had about 430 locomotives of 50 classes allocated to six sheds within 10 miles of the passenger termini. Add to this nearly 100 locomotives at Feltham, 15 miles out, and somewhere around 30% of the company's locomotives were in the London area. An even greater proportion of its classes could be seen in London, either as residents or visitors. Despite the secondary rôle of steam, the Southern could offer more than the Great Western, which was all steam!

The Great Western

The GWR was not really a 'London railway', despite having its head office in Paddington and its largest locomotive shed at Old Oak Common. There were more locomotives, classes, sheds, and main passenger stations within 10 miles of Cardiff than anywhere else on the system, while the more amorphous West Midlands district was also busier than London. However, if one discounts the company's interest in the Hammersmith & City line (operated by London Transport), and the rare appearance of a diesel railcar in Paddington, one could say the Great Western was fully steam operated in London.

There was but one terminus, Paddington, from which departed and arrived the principal passenger services serving the provinces. These were hauled almost entirely by various 4-6-0s from 'Kings' to 'Granges', only the 'Manors' being infrequent visitors. Medium-distance trains, even expresses, often had Mogul haulage. Alone of the four large main line companies, the 4-4-0 was a distinct rarity, although a few 'Dukedogs' were to be seen in the London district, and used mainly on local goods work for which 0-6-0s were more suitable.

Paddington's suburban service was mainly in the hands of the capable '61XX' 2-6-2T, all of which were allocated to the London district, although this extended out as far as Oxford. They can, therefore, be counted as a special London design. More so were the '9700' class 0-6-0PT with condensing apparatus for underground work, which spent their whole lives stationed at OOC on a wide variety of local work in addition to their subterranean sorties. There were, of course, numerous standard panniers of the '5700' and '8750' classes for shunting, empty stock work, and local goods trains, these classes being almost ubiquitous around London. There had to be an exception, as always on the GWR, and Southall shed had a rare saddle tank, No 1925, for working Hayes sleeper works.

The Great Western was probably the most branch line-minded company in the country. Even within the London suburban area to inner destinations off the main line, which other companies would run from their main termini, the GWR ran country-style branch lines, involving change of train. For these, Southall shed had a majority of the '54XX' auto-fitted 0-6-0PT, almost a London class, and to maintain the company policy of non-standard standardisation, there were a couple of the old '35XX' 2-4-0T, probably on standby service.

For variety and strangers, one had to keep an eye on the freight service, worked by provincial locomotives bringing in the goods to the metropolis, and departing home with empties. Both Old Oak Common and Southall had allocations of truly freight locomotives, of which the '47XX' class heavy 2-8-0 were the most notable, most of the class being London based. Heavy freight from the West, mainly South Wales, brought in many '28XX' 2-8-0s, Moguls and mixed traffic 4-6-0, these types handling perhaps 90% of the tonnage. The other 10% brought in the rarities: ROD 2-8-0s, 'Aberdares', '72XX' 2-8-2Ts, and even

Top left:
Condensing pannier No 9702, built especially for underground freight duties, approaches Acton station, rather surprisingly on the down main line. *A. E. Durrant*

Centre left:
The Great Western suburban in later days is typified by 'Large Prairie' No 6152 hurrying towards Paddington with five modern coaches. The background bridge carries the Willesden-Acton line, over which locomotives of the other three main line companies regularly ran. *A. E. Durrant*

Below:
Not untypical on the Western was a Mogul speeding through Acton with express headlamps up. No 7331 is one of the last batch with side window cabs, better known in GWR days as the '93XX' series. *A. E. Durrant*

Above:
The Great Western in London must include a 'King' photograph, in this case showing No 6010 *King Charles I* passing under the empty stock flyover at Old Oak Common on a Birmingham train.
A. E. Durrant

occasionally a 2-8-0T or a '56XX' 0-6-2T. Lighter and local freights could arrive behind a 'Duke', 'Bulldog' or 'Dukedog' 4-4-0, usually but not always from the outer reaches of the London Division, and there sometimes appeared, '2251' and '2301' class 0-6-0s, this type also being rare on the GWR, although common on other railways. The London Division, at Reading and Didcot, contained the last three (ex-MSWJR) 2-4-0s on the GWR, but I have no personal recollection of their presence in the inner London area; this being probably less likely than seeing an 'Aberdare' from Severn Tunnel Junction or Oxley.

In total, the GWR had about 300 locomotives allocated within 10 miles of Paddington, roughly 250 at Old Oak and 50 at Southall. These comprised only 15 classes, the most standard allocation in London, and was nearly equalled by the dozen classes which might be seen from time to time as visitors. In fact, if one includes 'foreign' visitors to Southall, locomotives arriving on freights from the former Great Central line, the visiting types outnumber the residents. These classes will be included under the Neasden (LNER) shed, although in fact it was common to see an 'O4', 'K3', 'B7' or rarer type on Southall shed on a Sunday afternoon.

The LMS

The LMS presence in London comprised basically the LNWR and the Midland. However, as the LNWR had previously absorbed the North London Railway, and the Midland the LT&SR, there were in the wartime 1940s locomotives and workings from four constituents at work within London. Similarly, the LMS operated from four London passenger termini, of which Euston and St Pancras were wholly company-operated, whilst Broad Street and Fenchurch Street were shared with the LNER. Somehow the LMS termini always seemed to be gloomier and foggier than those of the other companies, this perhaps being accentuated by the drab maroon of the coaching stock, made worse by wartime lack of cleaning, and by a general air of providing a reluctant service under sufferance, an attitude present in a lesser degree on the other three main lines.

Euston, of course, was the premier LMS station, probably to the disgust of the strong Midland management cadre, and this piecemeal terminus, set in a location which might be described as an open-air dungeon, saw the biggest technical variety of locomotives in London. At the top end of the scale were Stanier's superb 'Duchesses', invariably grubby, and in those early wartime days available in both streamlined and unstreamlined forms, the former in either blue or red liveries, just discernible under the grime. These were supplemented by the rather rare 'Princess Royal' class, and in theory by the 'Turbomotive', although I never saw this

working in wartime days. The basic heavy service was carried out by the 'Scots', all in original, parallel-boilered form, aided by 'Patriots' and 'Jubilees'. Stanier's Class 5s handled anything within their capacity, and trains from Bletchley often had 'Prince of Wales' 4-6-0s, including No 25845, the Walschaerts-fitted 'Tishy'.

Above:
At the top of Camden bank, 'Jubilee' No 45631 *Tanganyika* from Longsight thunders up with what is presumably a Manchester train, while 'Duchess' No 46236 *City of Bradford* awaits the signal to cross into the shed yard. *A. E. Durrant*

All in all, Euston's cramped situation made it a poor place for train watching, and even as a schoolboy it was soon discovered that Willesden Junction was far better. One tended to get there by the Euston-Watford LMS electric, with its sliding doors which could be opened when running to give better views of passing locomotives, but on rare occasions there would be a steam train stopping at Willesden, with the opportunity of travelling behind a Fowler 2-6-4T or, less frequently, a 'Prince of Wales' 4-6-0. At Willesden one could view with incredulity the locomotives entrusted with empty stock workings into the company's principal London terminus. Compared with the sturdy pannier tanks at Paddington, or the smart-looking 'E2s' at Victoria, here were antediluvian contrivances so small and low slung that even from the LNWR's fairly low platforms, a schoolboy could look over the top of the boiler! 'Like the *Rocket*' became less an insult and more a statement of fact! These little engines, nominally built by Webb, but really dating back to his predecessors, were the 'Cauliflower' 0-6-0, the 0-6-2T version thereof, and the smaller-wheeled 'Coal Tank' 0-6-2T. These tiny engines, all long chimneys and no boilers, must have caused many a passenger to wonder whether such a midget was actually going to haul him to his destination in the northern counties. Unfortunately, LMS operating was such that he probably blamed his inevitable late arrival on being hauled by 'the *Rocket*'!

St Pancras, with its high arched roof, somehow gave the impression of being aloof from wartime realities. Trains were infrequent, the biggest engines were 'Jubilees', while lesser species such as Class 5s, Compounds, or even '2P' 4-4-0s managed the traffic. Suburban trains were sometimes 2-6-4T, but often 2-6-2T, not the vigorous variety as used by the GWR, but the feeble Fowler version, of modern appearance but hopeless performance, such as would probably be bettered by the spindly 'Coal Tank' 0-6-2T at Willesden. Carriage pilot duties were mainly carried out by gentle Johnson 0-4-4Ts, and in the adjoining St Pancras freight sidings one could see the same designer's Class 1F 0-6-0T, some still with open-backed cabs, the only such tank engines in London. Perhaps the most archaic shunting power was the horse which, by means of ropes and capstans, shunted wagons of best Burton bitter beer on to the lift which descended to the cellars below.

Broad Street was the third LMS station, but for most of the day this high level edifice hosted only the fairly sparse electric train service over the former North London Railway. At peak hours, however, Broad Street got into steam with suburban trains from this City terminus to outer destinations. There were both LMS trains (usually with 2-6-4Ts to the former LNWR main line) and Gresley 'N2' 0-6-2T for GNR destinations. All these could be seen from the platform ends at adjacent Liverpool Street, while observing the busy GE scene. The fourth LMS-used terminus was at Fenchurch Street, actually owned by the LNER but allowing the LMS to use a couple of platforms. Services on the owning railway were relatively sparse, and hauled mainly by 'N7' 0-6-2Ts. How the LMS (formerly LT&SR) managed to cram its extensive service into two platforms was a miracle of operating expertise conspicuous by its absence elsewhere on that railway, particularly on the LNWR main line. Main motive power were the superb Stanier three-cylinder 2-6-4Ts which operated like clockwork, but these were still outnumbered by the larger boilered 'Tilbury' 4-4-2T, which looked rather like a tank version of a Midland Compound, whose masquerade was accentuated by the similar roaring exhaust and clanking rods.

Within the 10-mile radius of termini, the LMS had five locomotive sheds, at Camden, Willesden, Kentish Town, Cricklewood and Devons Road, and it was possible to see some 40 locomotive classes, of which about 35 classes were London residents. Despite its projected image of an efficient and highly standardised railway, the LMS was able to produce such exotica as the oldest working locomotive of a main line railway company (the 1858 0-4-2T at Bow Works) and as regular visitors, Britain's only main line haulage articulateds, in the form of the Garratts which entered Cricklewood yards from the Midlands.

Below:
Directly developed from Churchward's four-cylinder express locomotives were the LMS 'Princess Royal' class. No 46207 *Princess Arthur of Connaught* in maroon livery speeds towards Primrose Hill tunnel with an up express shortly before withdrawal.
A. E. Durrant

The LNER

This railway, operating out of three owned and one used termini, had the greatest steam presence in London in the days under review. It had the largest number of locomotives, the greatest variety of classes, a shed with the largest locomotive allocation the world has ever known, and was totally steam! The younger enthusiast generation of today simply cannot imagine a spectacle such as Liverpool Street station on a winter's evening rush hour, with 18 all-steam platforms each handling from four to 10 arrivals and departures, the constant clatter of incoming trains, mixed with the chugging of departures, smoke, steam and fog everywhere; hell perhaps for the mere passenger, but heaven for the steam enthusiast! And, as a perpetual background rhythm, the panting of a score of Westinghouse brake pumps. It is possible, perhaps, that Waterloo or Victoria stations before the start of electrification may have equalled Liverpool Street, but I suspect that this Great Eastern terminus was the busiest steam station the world has ever known. Certainly my mother (generally ignorant of railways) always knew when I had been to Liverpool Street, simply by the blackness of face, tonnage of grit in hair, and ecstatic expression of total consummation! What is more, all this was achieved by small locomotives, the biggest being the 'B17' 'Sandringhams', descending via 'K3s', 'B12s', 'Clauds', and a plethora of tank types from 'V1' class 2-6-2Ts, through countless 'N7' 0-6-2Ts, down to the surprisingly frequent 'F4', 'F5' and 'F6' class 2-4-2Ts which gallantly staggered out of Liverpool Street with 10-coach loads of articulated stock for such mysterious destinations as Loughton and Ongar.

King's Cross, always regarded as the LNER's top station in London, was certainly second in quantity and variety. Of course, it handled much more important trains, to more distant destinations than Liverpool Street, and here were to be seen the company's top locomotives: the Pacifics and 'V2s', while even secondary services merited Atlantics. Suburban trains had 0-6-2T Classes 'N1' and 'N2', both larger than the 'N7' which formed the backbone of the GE services. Empty stock often had the suburban 0-6-2T, frequently supported by Class J52 0-6-0ST, these being the only saddle tanks which could be seen regularly in any London passenger terminus. Of course, most people came to view the magnificent large main line locomotives, the 'A1' (original), 'A3' and 'A4' Pacifics, the 'V2' 2-6-2, the Ivatt Atlantics, but little else on the main line. With the heaviest trains in the country, the thrashings, slippings and strugglings of these engines as they tried to accelerate across a maze of greasy pointwork generated an indelible impression, in comparison with which the strident tones of Wagner's music seemed quite restrained.

The LNER's third terminus was Marylebone, the most provincial and least metropolitan of all London's termini. Both its main line and suburban services were provincial in loadings and frequencies, but as they were powered mainly by Robinson's handsome machines, it was worth sacrificing quantity for quality, although in a variety of classes, quantity was nevertheless evident. The most numerous class seen at Marylebone was the 'A5' 4-6-2T, the biggest and probably the best suburban engines used on the LNER at the time, but used on the lightest service, their sheer size preventing an appearance in the cramped conditions of the heavier and busier services. At peak hours these were supplemented by the even bigger Class L1 (later 'L3') 2-6-4T, while on very rare occasions one of the ex-Metropolitan tanks, 'L2' or 'M2' might be seen, more usually further out on freight duties.

Main line locomotives were occasionally Gresley 'A1' or 'V2', and frequently 'B17' of the 'Football' series. Plenty of Robinson power was to be seen on the secondary services, Class D11 'Directors', 'C4' Atlantics and assorted 4-6-0s of Classes 'B1', 'B3' (original poppet valve, and the Thompson rebuilt No 6166), plus the 'B7' class mixed-traffic locomotives. The inside-cylinder 'B8' class also penetrated from Annesley on goods trains, as did the 'O4' class 2-8-0, but these were more likely to be seen on Southall GWR shed than on Neasden. For local duties there were 'C13', 'N5' and 'J11' classes. The fourth LNER terminus was Fenchurch Street, a Great Eastern offshoot, and used by more LMS trains than it was by services of the owning company.

The massive LNER presence, the largest in London, was served by locomotive sheds at Stratford, King's Cross, Hornsey and Neasden, between which about 800 steam locomotives were allocated. These were divided into about 45 different classes, to which at least another 15 classes could be seen as fairly normal visitors.

Right:
Rightaway at King's Cross! With the seemingly inevitable bandy stance, a platform worker relays the guard's starting signal as the driver of 'A3' Pacific No 60066 *Merry Hampton* gets under way. The engine has a double Kylchap exhaust, but has yet to acquire smoke deflectors. A smokebox door burnt during a previous thrash has yet to be repainted by 'Top Shed'. *A. E. Durrant*

Below:
Action at Belle Isle. Class J50 0-6-0T No 68979 staggers asthmatically uphill on empty stock while a 'V2' rolls in with a fitted freight. In the background is the exhaust steam from a 'J52' saddle tank shunting the yard.
A. E. Durrant

Left:
Hatfield shed on the GN main line housed some Great Eastern 'N7s' for local branch line work. Here No 69692 makes a rare appearance on the main line with a pick-up goods train.
A. E. Durrant

Below left:
A clear winter's morning at Belle Isle sees record-breaking 'A4' No 60022 *Mallard* chattering up the gradient with the down 'Flying Scotsman'.
A. E. Durrant

Conclusion

Thus the London resident of those wartime days would have, stationed within 10 miles of the passenger termini, over 2,000 locomotives of about 150 different classes, to which might be added a further 40 or even 50 additional classes from provincial visitors.

On top of these were the smallish stud owned by London Transport, for ballasting and similar duties, and a considerable number of industrial locomotives, varying from the odd saddle tank at power stations and gasworks to the substantial rosters of Beckton gasworks and the Port of London Authority. These industrials and others must have run to 200 steam locomotives, making the total London resident steam population about 2,300 to 2,400 locomotives!

None of this information, of course, is new — it is simply that I do not think it has been evaluated and compiled before.

Having put all this together, and claimed London as being World Steam Centre number one, what are the other possible contenders? Obviously, nothing in Britain. Number two, from personal knowledge, must be Paris, probably less known as a steam centre than for its numerous better publicised attractions. Paris had, within a similar distance of 16 kilometres from the main termini, about a dozen steam sheds hosting perhaps 1,600 locomotives. Chicago? I simply do not know, but suspect that it might wrest second place from Paris, but cannot win the top spot from London.

Photographically, I cannot illustrate the period described above, but have used later photographs of the same engines in the same places, albeit by then under the ownership of a nationalised railway system. For this, I apologise, but my then youth, coupled with wartime restrictions, prevented me from photographing them with the right owner's initials.

Birds and Steam Trains

Colin Boocock

It is a warm summer afternoon. At the water's edge a heron rests on one leg, observing the surrounding tranquility. Behind it, a woodland of mixed deciduous trees stretches to either side, emitting a variety of bird song. Quiet, human voices echo suppressed excitement as a family follows a nature trail amongst the trees, while bees buzz among the wild flowers. A kingfisher flashes up a stream and disappears through the low arch of a stone bridge.

Then an approaching low rumble heralds the unmistakeable chiffa-chuffa-chiffa-chuffa exhaust of a small steam locomotive. A gleaming creature of shiny green paint, polished copper and brass trundles across the bridge with a good-length train of open-sided, four-wheel carriages full of tourists and day trippers.

This is the Shane's Castle Railway in Northern Ireland in the summer.

It is indeed a great pity that so many tourists miss visiting Ulster. The province contains so much beautiful countryside and coastline, so many fine buildings, quiet loughs, good fishing — and delightfully friendly people. On a normal quiet day the problems of the area can seem so far away.

The attraction of a steam railway nonetheless has led many a visitor to detrain at Antrim from one of Northern Ireland Railways' efficient diesel-electric units. Straight ahead from the station entrance one can walk along the Randalstown road for about a quarter of an hour, to reach the Shane's Castle estate entrance on the left. In the summer season the gates are open and a friendly smile in the small gatehouse acknowledges the modest entrance fee.

Shane's Castle itself is over 1¼ miles from the gate. To move visitors across the estate to the castle, Lord O'Neill has achieved a long-felt dream: he has had a 3ft-gauge steam railway laid for the purpose. Opened in 1971, the railway follows the estate roadway for most of the distance.

Far left:
Shane's Castle Railway No 3 is a 1949-built Barclay 0-4-0WT, originally supplied for the Irish Turf Board's railway feeding Portarlington power station. Now named *Shane* after one of Lord O'Neill's three sons, No 3 is the line's most used locomotive. It is seen at the Antrim end of the line being prepared for service on 2 September 1984. *Colin Boocock*

Below:
The first train of the day on the last day of the season stands at Shane's Castle station with No 3 at its head, waiting to return to Antrim on 2 September 1984.
Colin Boocock

Alongside the line's 'Antrim' station are the locomotive and carriage sheds and workshops. One of the two principal steam locomotives, No 3 *Shane*, is in steam and is being lovingly polished by the driver. We learn that the driver is also engineer to the line. Virtually single-handed, he has restored the two working steam locomotives. No 3 is a modern Barclay 0-4-0WT, built in 1949 for Bord-na-Mona who employed it on turf trains near Portarlington. It is a sister engine to *Irish Pete* on the Talyllyn Railway.

The other regular engine on the Shane's Castle Railway is a diminutive Peckett 0-4-0T from the British Aluminium Co's factory at Larne harbour. Now No 1 *Tyrone*, this 1904-built machine first saw service on the SCR in 1972. The table gives the dimensions of these two engines, and of the other locomotives at the site, including one of superb ancestry to be revealed before the end of this article!

Lined up alongside the single platform is a string of four-wheeled, open-sided carriages, some open-topped, some roofed. *Shane* is nosing up to the front coach and being coupled on. A helper checks that all passengers have their estate entry tickets. There is a 'pip' on the whistle, the regulator is opened a crack, and the train moves off.

Dropping downhill slightly, the line passes a semaphore signal from the former County Donegal Railways. The train curves right, crosses the roadway, and plunges into a dense copse of trees and bushes which border close to the line. Another bout of whistling heralds the train's emergence, to cross the drive again, from which point the line takes up a continuous roadside position. All the way, the train is dwarfed by tall trees of a wide variety. The engine is worked fairly lightly, it being quite large for the job in hand and fully master of its load. Some visitors wave down the train to stop at Millburn halt. The halt enables visitors to detrain and use a picnic site, or to go down to the shore of Lough Neagh, surely the United Kingdom's largest area of fresh water.

On leaving the halt, which is properly laid with a neat, single platform, the train humps slightly over the small stone bridge. Some way further through the woods the line passes more open land, and then veers away from the road, curving towards the left, soon to arrive at Shane's Castle station.

The station is an excellent feature of the railway. Its classic railway architecture sports a substantial, glazed platform awning, and incorporates a large tea room (which dispenses very good home-made fare). The

Right:
A surviving tower of Shane's Castle overlooks No 3 *Shane* as the 0-4-0WT runs round its train. *Colin Boocock*

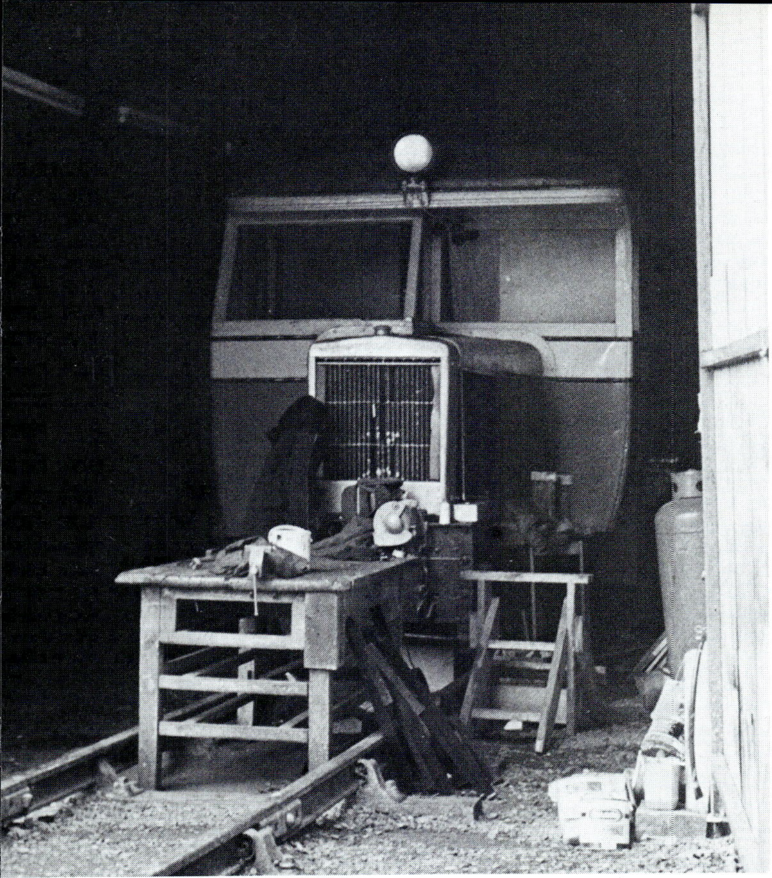

Left:
The County Donegal Railways Gardner-Walker railcar is seen stored in the depot.
Colin Boocock

Below:
This ex-British Aluminium Co 0-4-0T from Larne harbour is now No 1 *Tyrone* on the Shane's Castle Railway. *Colin Boocock*

inevitable tourist souvenir shop is housed in a most attractive, hip-roofed structure that came from the former NCC station at Portrush.

No 3 runs round its train here, but often people do not stop to watch. They have come to see the castle, and need only a short walk across a grassy field to reach it. The castle's history, while brief as castles go, is not without its moments of drama. The railway's excellent guide book, reveals much! Let us say that we have seen nothing like it anywhere else, that it almost borders the lough, and must surely have been haunted (by a Banshee?), let alone burned down twice. The visitor has plenty on which to exercise his imagination!

A railway enthusiast can spend a very pleasant afternoon walking slowly back along the roadway, photographing the train as it passes on its long series of runs shuttling visitors between the gate and the

Number	1	2	3	4	5	6
Name:	*Tyrone*	*Rory*	*Shane*	*Nippy*	*Nancy*	*Columbkille*
Builder:	Peckett	Simplex	Barclay	Hibberd	Avonside	Nasmyth-Wilson
Built:	1904	1956	1949	1936	1908	1908
Works No:	1026	11039	2265	2014	1547	?
Wheel arrangement:	0-4-0T	0-4-0D	0-4-0WT	0-4-0D	0-6-0T	2-6-4T
Wheel diameter:	1ft 8in	1ft 5in	2ft 0in	1ft 4in	2ft 10in	4ft 0in
Cylinders:	7in×10in	(3)	8.5in×12in	(2)	10in×18in	14in×21in
Boiler pressure:	150lb/sq in	—	180lb/sq in	—	160lb/sq in	175lb/sq in
Tractive effort:	3,332lb	—	5,527lb	—	6,260lb	12,755lb
Weight:	7 tons	7 tons	11 tons	4 tons	19 tons	43 tons
Engine:	—	Dorman	—	National	—	—
Horsepower:	—	50	—	?	—	—

castle. Photogenic whatever the light, the brilliant burnishing of the engine's metal parts is possibly without parallel in the British Isles; the woodland is a delightful place in which to be; and the atmosphere throughout the estate is one of relaxed friendliness.

Back at the main gate, one is reminded of an earlier occasion when, by invitation, we toured the locomotive and carriage sheds. It is truly remarkable that the engineering of two such superbly restored locomotives can have been undertaken here. Facilities are adequate, but certainly neither lavish nor ideal.

There are some gems hidden away in the depths of the shed and yard. Two diesels, a Simplex and a Planet, are available for line maintenance work. There is an Avonside 0-6-0T (No 1547 of 1908) called *Nancy*, yet to be restored and which came from an English iron ore line. But pride of place must go to the County Donegal Railways stock which is housed here.

The red 2-6-4T *Columbkille* last saw service in 1959. The author fondly remembers seeing her on cross-border freight workings shortly before the closure; and he remembers riding on Gardner-Walker railcars such as the pair now at Antrim. They look like buses but their cabs sit on the leading bogies which have coupling rods, and the drivers have no steering wheels to handle — altogether odd vehicles to behold! It is said that once a year their owners bring them out for a run to Shane's Castle. Long may they all survive.

In preparing this short article the author has unashamedly lifted facts and figures from the railway's published guidebook, which he hereby acknowledges, and has drawn on his memory of a splendid day's visit to this lovely place. He hopes that many others will venture to Antrim on a summer weekend and see for themselves how trees, a lough, birds, a castle and a steam train can together form such a memorable experience.

Above:
No 3 *Shane* takes a train of day trippers past Millburn halt as the line runs along the estate drive.
Colin Boocock

Right:
The two active steam locomotives of the SCR are seen at the depot near the main gate at the Antrim end of the line. No 1 *Tyrone*, built in 1904 by Peckett of Bristol, is dead inside the shed whilst No 3 *Shane* raises steam outside. *Colin Boocock*

Nigel Gresley and the Booster

G. J. Hughes BSc (Econ) C Eng FIEE

The highest overall efficiency of any form of machine is obtained in conditions of continuous operation against a constant load, at constant speed. The varied duties of the steam locomotive in everyday service placed it well outside such ideal considerations: its full capability was necessarily well above the usual demands made upon it. Most locomotive designers — but there were some well-known exceptions — believed that the maximum performance of a locomotive depended upon the capacity of its boiler to raise steam. A locomotive at starting may need all the power it can exert; owing to its low initial speed it will call for far less steam than the maximum the boiler is capable of supplying. So it has occurred to engineers that by providing a supplementary engine, this surplus steam could be utilised, and the locomotive given a 'boost' at starting.

The first recorded example of this being applied in practice was in 1865, when Beyer Peacock fitted an auxiliary engine (described as a 'steam bogie') to the pony truck of a 2-4-2 locomotive exported to the Tudela & Bilbao Railway of Spain. No record survives of its performance, and the experiment does not appear to have been repeated until 1896, when Krauss of Munich introduced a more sophisticated version on a locomotive constructed for the Bavarian State Railways. In this example, the auxiliary cylinders drove on to a pair of wheels of similar diameter to the bogie wheels, and which could be lowered on to the rails, and subsequently retracted, at the discretion of the driver. The same firm exhibited a further version at the Paris Exhibition of 1900; in this locomotive the centre wheels of a six-wheel bogie were driven by auxiliary cylinders and also could be raised or lowered at will. Nothing more has been traced of the subsequent history of these experimental machines.

Sturrock's well-known steam tenders, coupled to several of his 0-6-0 locomotives on the Great Northern Railway in the 1860s, were intended not so much as a booster, but to supplement the locomotive's tractive effort in

ordinary traffic, and were more akin to later Garratt developments. It will be recalled that these steam tenders led to protests by the enginemen, and were probably a factor in Sturrock's premature departure from the GNR. The same increase in output could have been obtained from greater cylinder volume and strengthening of components, which would have obviated the crews' objections. But mere dimensional increase is not the way of the innovator.

It is hard to believe that the inventive Americans did not introduce the booster at an earlier date, but this seems not to have been until just after World War 1, when the device was rediscovered and applied to a New York Central Atlantic. Possibly this delay in applying the booster in the USA arose from earlier extensive use of the 4-4-0 and 4-6-0 types, in preference to the 4-4-2. Later developments, following the application of the wide firebox, favoured the 4-6-2 and 4-8-2 types in preference to the 4-8-0, and the presence of a trailing pony truck provided the designer with a chassis on which an auxiliary engine could be mounted. Once proved in traffic conditions, the device sold in large numbers, and within 10 years 3,000 locomotives in the USA were fitted with boosters.

As Locomotive Superintendent of the Great Northern Railway in England, Nigel Gresley appreciated the potential of the booster. The increasing loads of the GNR long-distance expresses were beginning to exceed the capabilities of the Ivatt Atlantics, improved though they were through the refinements of superheating and piston valves. In 1922, Gresley had his first two Pacifics in traffic, but multiplication of the design was still some distance in the future. So in September of that year he put a proposal to the GNR Locomotive Committee that because of difficulties with trains exceeding 14 coaches, and with engines stalling between King's Cross and Holloway, a set of booster equipment should be purchased from the Franklin Railway Supply Co of the USA for $5,200 and fitted to one of the large Atlantics for trial purposes. At the then current exchange rate, this was equivalent to about £1,000. The expenditure was agreed, and Oliver Bulleid was placed in charge of the project.

The booster was bought as a standard item from the American manufacturers and, in that land of powerful locomotives, was probably one of the smallest available off the shelf. It consisted of two double-acting non-reversible 10in×12in cylinders with piston valves, driving the 3ft 8in trailing wheels of the Atlantic through spur gearing. In line with US practice, compressed air was used to put the gears into mesh, against a spring which normally held them apart. The booster theoretically increased the locomotive's tractive effort by half, from 17,450lb to 25,950lb. (Because of the pressure drop along the long steam pipe, the booster's tractive effort was calculated at 71½% of the nominal boiler pressure.) To accommodate the assembly, the Atlantic's frames were lengthened, and prominent steam pipes were provided externally to supply the booster's cylinders and to convey the exhaust steam to the smokebox. Also, a Westinghouse pump was fitted to provide compressed air to operate the mechanism. The elongated frames enabled a Pacific type cab to be fitted, and as a result the locomotive selected for the conversion, No 1419 (LNER No 4419) was the only Great Northern Atlantic to possess a cab of adequate length, and with the comfort of side windows.

The conversion completed, Bulleid was able to report that the Atlantic could start anywhere, and with 535 tons behind the tender could give

Left:
Ivatt Large Atlantic No 4419 as rebuilt by Gresley with a booster on the trailing wheels of the locomotive.
Real Photographs

Right:
An unusual rear three-quarter view of No 4419, showing clearly the modified trailing truck which was fitted with two 10in × 12in cylinders.
Ian Allan Library

increased acceleration. This statement was perhaps a little generous, but certainly 18 coaches, some no doubt lighter in weight than the contemporary East Coast standard, were lifted up the 1 in 105 to Holloway and onwards up the 1 in 200 to Potters Bar. However, it soon became obvious that even the gutsy Atlantic boiler could not provide enough steam to keep the booster going for long, and it had to be cut out to prevent the boiler from becoming drained. Moreover, at starting from King's Cross, the boiler was, in railwaymen's terms, 'cold'. But this was not all. The increased unsprung weight at the end of the locomotive, now 18 tons on the trailing wheels, caused considerable oscillation, which added to the enginemen's reaction to this uncertain technology, and did not endear No 4419 to its crews. However for a time it appears to have taken its turns on the heaviest Great Northern expresses, normally only using the booster at starting.

A later report, prepared after the booster had been in service for a couple of years, was more realistic. Whilst acknowledging the benefit of greater tractive effort when it was most needed, at starting, further drawbacks were described. As there was no separate regulation of the steam supply to the booster, it could only be operated with the same degree of control as the main engine, that is, at starting, in full gear. Despite the greater adhesion weight on the trailing wheels, these tended to slip badly. Then, if the train would not start, the driver attempted to set back, the main engine would be in reverse but the booster, which could only act in the forward direction, would act in opposition. To set back, in fact, the driver had first to disengage the booster, which took some time as the steam in its cylinders had to be dissipated. In addition to these operating difficulties, trouble was also experienced with leaking steam joints, particularly at the flexible pipes on the trailing truck, which added to the crews' discomfort by filling the cab with steam. The compressed air supply also seems to have been a source of irritation.

In 1925 Darlington Works carried out a remarkable piece of machining by replacing the original 14-tooth gearwheel by one with 24 teeth, so increasing the crankshaft speed proportionally. This was intended to enable the booster to be engaged at speeds of up to 25mph. This also had the converse effect of reducing the supplementary tractive effort to 4,970lb, but this was not considered a disadvantage as slipping under full throttle had prevented the original theoretical figure of 8,500lb from being used effectively. However, the new arrangement did not reduce the demand for steam, and by now it was realised that if the booster was to be employed successfully, a correct relationship would have to be worked out between steam requirements and steam supply, and appropriate alterations made. In fact it was calculated that the steam required with the main engine in full gear, and the booster in operation, was equivalent to the needs of two 24in×24in cylinders, instead of the 20in×24in of the standard piston valve Atlantic. Nothing, however, was done to increase the overall steam supply, although an even larger boilered Atlantic would have been an interesting project, and Doncaster drawing office completed some preliminary work on such a proposal. Some improvements were carried out to the draughting, in order to get the exhaust steam away more quickly, and the compressed air operation of the engaging mechanism was replaced by steam. Further tests, this time with the dynamometer car, demonstrated the locomotive's capabilities under trial conditions, including drawing away from a signal stop on the 1 in 96 of Cockburnspath bank, between Edinburgh and Berwick, which would have been impossible without the booster. In later passenger train operation the locomotive was

Left:
A fascinating photograph of the cab of No 4419, with the rear of the booster-fitted truck clearly visible.
Locomotive Publishing Co

Below:
No 4419 at speed with a six-coach Pullman train. The clean, attractive lines of the design were somewhat spoiled by the pipework associated with the booster modification. *P. Ransome-Wallis*

employed between Leeds and Doncaster, when the booster was said to have been very useful, giving rapid acceleration from intermediate stops; but no doubt mechanical unreliability and general dislike of the device led to its disuse, and final removal in 1935.

Despite the lack of real success with No 4419, which must have been known by the Chief General Manager and the Board, in 1929 a further proposal was submitted for an express passenger class to be provided with a booster, using a similar argument to that which had been employed six years before. This time the subject was the North Eastern 'Z' class Atlantic, LNER Class C7. It was claimed that whilst these locomotives could successfully haul trains of medium weight, double heading had often to be resorted to. Provision of a booster would enable heavier loads to be hauled, particularly up Cockburnspath, a route on which the 'C7' was regularly employed. Since several of the class were in need of reboilering, a case was prepared for two examples to be fitted with boosters. Each of the locomotives would be provided with a larger capacity boiler, and the additional rear-end weight would be carried on a bogie articulating the engine with its tender. The booster cylinders were to be 10½in×14in, larger than those fitted to the 'C1' conversion, but the drive would have a 1:1 ratio. The additional tractive effort was put at 5,000lb, that of the locomotive itself being 22,012lb. The booster no longer had to be imported, as a British manufacturer, J. Stone & Co Ltd of Deptford, was prepared to supply, but required an order for a minimum of five. Gresley, having in mind also applying boosters to three 0-8-4 shunting tanks, considered this package to be satisfactory at a price of around £875 per set of equipment, so that although five were ordered, they were of two different sizes.

The costing included in the proposal made the best of the circumstances. Although, in addition to the booster itself, and its ancillary hardware, a new and enlarged boiler, new tender, and an articulated bogie were to be provided, full credit was allowed for the replacement boiler not now needed, the existing tender, only partially written off, and the trailing wheels, which were no longer required and could be held as spare. So the net estimated cost was no more than £1,450 — although, in the event, the work cost double the estimate. A good deal of unforeseen difficulty was experienced in the design and fitting of the booster, but this was surmounted in time, and the two conversions, Nos 727 and 2171, re-entered traffic from Darlington at the end of 1931.

The classification of the rebuilds posed an interesting problem: were they still Atlantics, or were they more correctly 4-4-4-4s, and if so were they tank engines? Any purist notions of observing the niceties of the Whyte notation were soon dispelled by the CME: the engines were still Atlantics, and that was that. So they were reclassified as 'C9s', a class number considerately left vacant between the North Eastern and North British series of Atlantics when the LNER classification list was drawn up in 1923. In any case, the scheme had no spare letters to cover new wheel arrangements, apart from 'I', which had been deliberately omitted to avoid confusion with the figure '1'.

In service, the two 'C9' class locomotives seem to have been capable of better starting, but not of improved haulage up the steep banks. Perhaps the length of time between conception and completion reacted to their disadvantage, and with 20 years' service under their belts, the 'C7s' as a class might have been regarded as having their best years behind them. Anyway, after no more than five years, the boosters were removed, and unusually — but perhaps because he had been asked to do so by a critical Locomotive Committee — Gresley reported that the experiment had not been entirely successful. The Directors were informed that the load handled by the 'C9s' was limited to that which they were able to start on Cockburnspath, should they be brought to a stop by a signal. It was found that with heavier trains, whilst there was a drop in speed up the bank, it did not fall as low as 27mph, the highest speed at which the booster could be brought into operation. If the train was travelling as slowly as this, it was losing time anyway; moreover, the booster could not be disengaged at a speed much higher than 30mph. So, the lessons of No 4419 were learnt over again.

The application of the booster to main line freight locomotives was no more successful than in the passenger locomotive adaptions, but for different reasons. In this case, although the overall design was better proportioned, the project was insufficiently thought through. The run on which the booster-fitted locomotives were to be employed was the haulage of coal from the concentration yards at New England, Peterborough, to the distribution point at Ferme Park, Hornsey. This was a remunerative part of LNER operations; long, loose-coupled trains of loaded privately-owned wagons trundling slowly up to London, returning empty after having discharged their coal into the merchants' depots. In addition to locally distributed coal, there were also transits to the South-East, via the Metropolitan system and New Cross, as well as for power stations and gas works and 'Loco Coal Only' wagons for King's Cross and Hornsey sheds. In later years a feature of many of these long trains were the 50-ton vacuum braked bogie brick wagons, one of which would be marshalled immediately behind the locomotive, providing additional braking power.

The superheated version of Ivatt's 'Long Tom' 0-8-0s could deal comfortably with a haul of 60 wagons, aggregating 1,000 tons loaded. This was increased to 80 wagons and 1,300 tons with Gresley's first 2-8-0 design, his '01' of 1913, followed in 1918 by his 3-cylinder version, the more efficient '02'. These designs were replicated in 1919-1924, when a further 40 were built, a sufficient number to work the bulk of the Ferme Park coal traffic, which they continued to do until the arrival of the 'Austerities' towards the end of World War 2.

It may seem strange in retrospect that the LNER, always looking for further ways of reducing costs, should not have tackled these coal hauls more energetically in an effort to improve their efficiency. The main problem, of course, was that the railway was merely acting as carrier for a variety of coal owners and merchants, hauling privately-owned wagons which were filled at the pithead and emptied at their destination by non-railway personnel. Another consideration was the configuration of the LNER main line, four-tracked only in parts, so that the slow mineral trains were often held at the commencement of two-tracked sections until faster trains had passed. Presumably any substantial improvement would have called for track reconstruction which would have been impossible to fund in the circumstances of the company's financial position, as well as the provision of continuous-braked wagons, which would have required a revolution in the practices of the private owners.

It was against this background that Gresley conceived his 2-8-2 'P1' class, which was calculated to be capable of increasing the haul to 100 loaded wagons, 1,600 tons; assuming a fleet of these new locomotives, the number of train movements to move a given tonnage would be reduced by one-fifth. With his pride of achievement in his newly introduced Pacifics, Gresley clearly visualised the application of similar basic design features — large boiler, wide firebox, three cylinders with conjugated valve gear, to a massive freight locomotive. He was determined to demonstrate to the traffic department that he could provide the engines, and it

Left:
The conversion by Gresley of two Class C7 Raven Atlantics with a booster-fitted four-wheel truck articulated with the tender produced one of the most peculiar designs to operate in regular service in Britain. Although the new class could scarcely be described as remaining an Atlantic, the LNER persisted in describing it thus, the two rebuilt locomotives becoming Class C9. No 727 is seen in works grey livery. *Ian Allan Library*

Below left:
The only other example of Class C9 was No 2171. The expense and complication involved with the rebuilding of the two locomotives was not justified by the limited improvement in performance. After only five years in service the boosters were removed and the experiment was abandoned. *Photomatic*

was up to them to provide the trains. The fact that they could not was no concern of his. But it ought to have been the concern of the management, and here we come again to one of the curiosities of the LNER organisation. Although the committee structure was such that the Divisional Superintendent, responsible for train operation, would have been aware of the genesis of the Mikado, there is no record of any representation on his part that he would be unable to use the locomotive to its full capability. Unbraked, loose-coupled trains of the length projected were unwieldy and hazardous, and not all the passing loops were long enough to cope with them. Nevertheless Gresley, intent on keeping in front of traffic demands, pressed ahead with his plans, which were presented to the LNER Locomotive Committee in August 1923. His proposal was to build at an estimated cost of £8,000 each (excluding the booster, which was not mentioned at this stage) two of a new type of heavy coal engine, to work between London and Doncaster, and between Wath and Immingham. (There is, however, no evidence that they ever worked regularly other than between Peterborough and London.) Whatever the operating people might or might not have thought, Gresley had the foresight in April 1923 to consult the Civil Engineer, who intimated that he had no objection to the locomotives on the score of weight. Undoubtedly the Chairman, William Whitelaw, would also have sought such reassurance, for only eight years before, whilst running the Highland Railway, he had been concerned in removing from his post their Locomotive Engineer, F. G. Smith, who, in building his 'River' class 4-6-0s had omitted to consult the Civil Engineer beforehand, which was unfortunate as they were deemed to be too heavy for the Highland main line of the time.

And so the two massive 'P1s' were built, No 2393 emerging from Doncaster in time to participate in the 1925 Centenary parade, followed by No 2394 later that year. The estimate of £8,000 each was considerably understated as they came out at £20,986 for the pair, at a time when ex-WD Robinson 2-8-0s were being bought for £1,500 each, plus reconditioning. Evidently, as is frequently the

case with prototypes, constructional difficulties arose, although the two Mikados immediately followed the second production batch of Pacifics, which they resembled in many dimensions.

The boosters appear to have been an afterthought, as they were omitted from the original costing, and were not mentioned in the submission to the Locomotive Committee. Similar in pattern to that fitted to No 4419, and also operated by compressed air, the boosters were intended to assist in starting, and when nearing the summits of the long 1 in 200 banks which are such a feature of the Great Northern main line. Use of the booster increased the tractive effort of the 'P1s' from 38,500lb to around 47,000lb, whilst the Diagram 94 boiler common to the Mikados and the original Pacifics was evidently man enough to provide the additional steam required for short periods. However, mechanical troubles with the boosters plagued the 'P1s'; a particularly serious problem arising from fractures of the casting forming the manifold connection for the steam circuit, a situation aggravated by the small radius of the curves on the triangle used for turning at New England, the depot not possessing a 70ft turntable at the time when the engines were introduced. So they spent abnormally long periods out of action awaiting the manufacture of special parts. The lost time would have been materially lessened had spare parts been made available in advance, but there are indications that New England was quite happy to manage without the 'P1s'.

In his original proposals, Nigel Gresley had claimed that this new design would be capable of handling 25% more loaded wagons than the 'O2' class, the normal load for which was 80 wagons. (In fact, on test a 'P1' was found to be able to start 2,040 tons on level track, compared with 1,660 tons for an O2, an increase of 19%.) But to run trains of this length in everyday service introduced problems which ought to have been foreseen, and the operational difficulties soon began to be aired. It was accepted that the Mikados could handle 100

Top:
No 2393 heads a lengthy rake of private owner coal wagons at Hadley Wood. The resemblance to the early Gresley Pacifics is apparent.
Locomotive Publishing Co

Left:
In contrast to the modifications carried out on the former GNR and NER Atlantics, the two Class P1 2-8-2 freight locomotives were built new with booster equipment. No 2394 shows the powerful lines of this handsome design.
Ian Allan Library

wagons, but the trains were too long for many of the loops and sidings, they occupied track circuits which slowed down following trains, and in certain locations could even run over into three block sections.

A special link was formed at New England to crew the engines but, even so, complaints were made by enginemen and guards that they had difficulty in carrying out working rules and regulations, particularly since the two ends of the train were often out of sight of each other. Coal consumption of the Mikados was reported to be over 130lb per mile, heavy enough, but having regard to the class of train and its slow and interrupted progress, perhaps not so bad on a lb/dbhp/hr basis. The fireman would have had plenty of time to shovel the four tons or so of coal consumed by the engine as it made its way along, often taking as much as seven hours on the journey, of which one-third would be spent waiting at signals. However this rate of coal consumption was evidently no more than that of the LMS Beyer-Garratts which later worked the Midland line mineral traffic between Toton and Brent.

Had the LNER possessed higher capacity coal wagons, particularly if they had been fitted with continuous brakes, and had been capable of higher speeds, so that greater payload could have been packed into a shorter train and run at a speed more commensurate with the design's capability, the outcome would have been different. But this would have called for a radically new approach to the whole question of this class of traffic movement, with vast reinvestment by the railway and the coal industry, and the 1920s were not a propitious period for solving problems of this nature.

Gresley had demonstrated that he could build a powerful, large freight engine, in the forefront of the technology of the day; Oliver Bulleid regarded the design as one of his favourites, and the locomotive world had to wait a further 30 years until another locomotive of this calibre appeared, this time of the 2-10-0 type, built to Austerity standards in World War 2. But the Mikados were ahead of their time, and their trailing loads were reduced to 90, and then 80 wagons, so meeting operating convenience and taking away the need for the boosters, which were removed in the mid-1930s. The locomotives themselves were the first Gresley products to be scrapped (other than 'A4' No 4469, which was withdrawn as a result of severe damage sustained in an air raid in 1942), their withdrawal date being July 1945; just 20 years after their emergence from Doncaster.

Nigel Gresley's final application of the booster was more successful, and although the particular boiler was not designed with a booster in mind, the locomotive operating cycle was such that more reasonable results could be obtained. The class was the GCR Robinson 0-8-4T, LNER Class S1, originating from 1907, when the first of a batch of four was turned out by Beyer Peacock. These were used for hump shunting duties at Wath marshalling yard, and had been steadily at work for over 20 years, when Gresley, considering at the same time the conversions of the two 'C7' Atlantics, decided to provide one of the existing 'S1s' with a booster, and to build two new engines so fitted, all to work at Wath and releasing two unconverted 'S1s' to shunt the new yard at Whitemoor. Added to the two booster equipments concurrently in mind for the 'C7s', this made up the package of five which were bought from J. Stone & Co. However, a new feature was incorporated in the boosters applied to the 'S1s'. Following reports of successful trials in 1929 on the Santa Fe Railroad with a booster fitted with a gearbox providing a reverse drive, the three boosters for the 'S1s' were specified with this refinement. At this distance in time, no reason can be deduced for this; in fact, the locomotive always humped with the smokebox leading, returning downhill backwards as light engine, and in the ordinary course of events never straying on to a turntable or triangle. Consequently they never required the refinement of the booster operating in reverse, and the provision of the reverse gear seems to have been pointless. Indeed, the boosters fitted to the two production 'S1s' were rendered incapable of operation in reverse before the locomotives were placed in traffic. A further unique feature was the coupling of the trailing bogie wheels, which to the purist would present the engines as of the 0-8-4-0T wheel arrangement. However, as with the 'C9' class previously discussed, the down-to-earth Gresley would have none of this nonsense, and the engines remained described as 0-8-4T, not even achieving a new class number. The booster-fitted variants were merely awarded part numbers as 'S1/2' for the rebuild (No 6171) and 'S1/3' for the new engines, Nos 2798/99, which were also provided with boilers slightly modified from the originals. The 'S1s', in common with most Robinson products, were robust engines, and possessed three 18in×26in cylinders and slide valves operated by individual sets of Stephenson motion. The only concession to providing the booster-fitted locomotives with greater boiler capacity was to fit superheaters, but since the engine's operating pattern was one of short bursts of full output followed by periods of inaction, the likelihood of their becoming winded was fairly remote.

Tractive effort was calculated at 34,523lb (at the time of building they were the most powerful main line locomotives in Britain) to which the booster, with its 10in×12in cylinders, added a theoretical 12,373lb, an increase of over one-third. This was sufficient to justify its introduction on the grounds that in bad weather the original 'S1s' had to be used in pairs, an expense avoided by the employment of the booster. Moreover, it was claimed that in favourable circumstances the boosters enabled the locomotives to propel 1,100 tons up the hump, compared with only 750 tons for the unfitted engines. All three booster-fitted 'S1s' were at work at Wath in 1932, the two new engines having been built at Gorton.

The boosters seem to have been successful in service, with the engines not requiring long periods of out-of-the-ordinary shopping, but use of the boosters had been discontinued by the early years of the war, and they were removed in 1943. Probably by then essential parts needed renewal, and replacements were impossible to obtain. No doubt the low speeds at which the 'S1s' normally operated contributed to the relative success of the boosters in this case, but no further engines were converted, nor was the experiment tried at any of the other LNER hump yards.

In retrospect, the booster seems to have been unsuccessful on the long-distance express engines for which it was mainly needed. Had it proved possible to apply it effectively to the pre-grouping Atlantic classes, these would have played an even more important part in the passenger services of the 1920s and 1930s. But unlike US practice in which the frames, boiler and booster were conceived as an entity at the original design stage, both the Atlantic conversions suffered from design inadequacies and mechanical shortcomings. The one class in which the booster attained reasonable success was in the least likely prospect, the large shunting tank, in contrast to US practice in which the main line engine was frequently provided with a booster, but the switcher hardly ever.

Below:
'P1' Mikado No 2394 storms past Potters Bar summit with a train of no fewer than 102 wagons. Unfortunately the usefulness of such haulage capacity was somewhat limited, particularly as a result of the limited capacity of loops and sidings.
Real Photographs

In Britain, Gresley was the only engineer to apply the booster in practice. The reasons why none of the CMEs of the other railways did so were twofold: locomotives suitable for conversion were few, but, more importantly, the initiative to build a new locomotive on US lines, incorporating a booster, was entirely lacking. The technology was reviewed by Oliver Bulleid in a Paper to the Institution of Locomotive Engineers in January 1928, during Gresley's first period as President, but the Paper evoked little discussion. Earlier, in May 1927, A. C. Stamer, Vincent Raven's erstwhile Assistant, and at that time the LNER Chief Assistant Mechanical Engineer, had read a Paper on the subject to the Association of Railway Locomotive Engineers. This was somewhat critical; he was probably aware of Gresley's intentions for the 'C7s' and was not wholly in favour.

The booster saga is an outstanding example of Nigel Gresley's continuing search for ways to improve locomotive efficiency. If the original conception had been followed by a more practical appraisal of its likely effectiveness, it might never have been introduced to this country, which would have saved the LNER a few thousand pounds, but would have denied the chance to assess the device in service.

Acknowledgements: Material for this article has been obtained from original LNER sources, and from the Archives of the Institution of Mechanical Engineers (Mr S. G. Morrison, Librarian). I am also grateful to Mr T. C. B. Miller for guidance on certain technical matters, and to Mr W. B. Yeadon and Mr M. G. Boddy for constructive criticism and assistance on details. Commentary however is entirely my own.

Below:
The final design to which Gresley fitted booster equipment was the former Great Central Railway 0-8-4T of Class S1. Two locomotives were built new in this form, whilst a third example was rebuilt from the existing 'S1' design. One of the new engines, No 2798, is seen in works grey livery. *LNER*

Bottom:
No 2798 is seen in service at Wath. The coupling rod fitted to the axles of the trailing bogie can be clearly seen. This was the most successful of Gresley's experiments with the booster system, but nonetheless the equipment was removed from the three locomotives in 1943 due to problems of spares and maintenance. *Ian Allan Library*

Nostalgia on the Southern

C. R. L. Coles

A recent journey along part of the M25 motorway recalled vivid and lasting memories of my only journey on one of several branch lines in southern England which became extinct in the early 1960s. But of this, more in a moment.

Ramblers' specials, walking tour tickets, hikers' mystery tours — these were but a few of the inexpensive travel bargains offered by the 'Big Four' during the 1930s. For the younger generation, whose incomes were in the lower pay brackets, such bargains proved immensely popular particularly for those who, after a week's work in the office or factory, wanted to enjoy a day in the country at a price well within their weekly budget.

You could pick up leaflets at most stations in the London area giving full details of these bargains which were based on a then well advertised slogan — 'There and back in the day for the price of the single fare'. The Southern Railway went even one better than that. With its network of closely integrated routes serving some of the most beautiful parts of England south of the River Thames, you were not obliged to return from the same station to which you had booked, nor even by

Left:
Ex-SECR 'D' class 4-4-0 No 1075 at Stewarts Lane depot in 1939. *C. R. L. Coles*

the same route. If you so wished, you could elect to return from any other station (not necessarily on the same route) on payment of the difference, if any, between the respective day return fares. These facilities became popularly known as 'Go as you please' tickets and proved a boon to ramblers and, as I soon discovered, to the railway connoisseur.

At that time far fewer people owned cars than is the case today. Thus, roads, particularly in country areas, were much less congested than now. Indeed, the now all too familiar motorway was not even dreamed of. For many the urge was to take full advantage of such bargains in order to get off the beaten track for a few hours and enjoy fully the many beauties of nature which the Almighty has given us. On almost any weekend or bank holiday, ramblers and the like (and these sometimes included railway enthusiasts) were to be seen in plenty at any Southern Railway terminal station bound for a day in the country, and it was on a fine, sunny January morning that I joined a small party at Victoria station. Where we would end up, nobody at that time knew and nobody really cared. A train would shortly be departing for stations to Tunbridge Wells and, being steam-hauled, we elected to travel on this train as far as Oxted where, before setting off on our walk, we closely inspected the locomotive whilst its tanks were being replenished with water. At that time new Maunsell side-corridor stock had begun to replace the older, somewhat less comfortable pre-Grouping non-corridor stock on certain routes in the Central division, but had yet to appear on the Oxted line. It was therefore a rake of these older vehicles which formed our train. The compartments seated five aside on each row and the luggage racks were, compared with those on new stock, somewhat narrower, with consequently more limited carrying capacity. Motive power was also of pre-Grouping origin, supplemented by Maunsell Class N Moguls.

We decided to follow the undulating slopes of the Greensand Ridge — a narrow belt of relatively high ground stretching eastwards from Oxted over a distance of about 12 miles, which separates the North Downs from the Kentish Weald. Ide Hill and Toys Hill, both properties of the National Trust, and which are a part of this ridge, are more than 700ft above sea level, the highest points in Kent, and command exquisite panoramic views of the Weald. From here we dropped down into Westerham, which at that time was served by the branch line from Dunton Green. During the 1930s this branch was very popular with

Above left:
'H2' 4-4-2 No 32425 *Trevose Head* on the 5.40pm service from London Bridge to East Grinstead near Upper Warlingham on 23 May 1952.
C. R. L. Coles

Left:
'N' class 2-6-0 No 1850 in malachite green livery, photographed near Sanderstead with a three-coach Maunsell set on a Tunbridge Wells-Victoria train in 1946. *C. R. L. Coles*

GUARD
31875

rambling clubs (both as a starting or finishing point), largely because of the exceptionally attractive country in this part of Kent.

Historically, Westerham is best known as being, since 1924, the country home of the late Sir Winston Churchill whose house, Chartwell, lies two miles south of the town. Here can be seen the various rooms as they existed during his lifetime as well as the garden studio containing many of Sir Winston's paintings. Also to be seen at Westerham is Quebec House, a gabled 17th century residence where General Wolfe, one of England's greatest soldiers, spent his early years. Both Chartwell and Quebec House are now owned by the National Trust. Pitt's Cottage, a half-timbered residence alleged to date from the 13th century (but much shored up by brick at a later date) was once the home of William Pitt. In recent years Pitt's Cottage became a restaurant (and to the best of my knowledge still is) and it was here that we enjoyed a delicious cream tea before moving on to Westerham station where, for those railway enthusiasts among our party, the climax of the day was to come. There must have been an exceptionally large number of ramblers that day because, as the departure time drew close, it was standing room only — even in the brake van! Not until reaching Dunton Green to await the next train to Charing Cross did we have an opportunity to inspect the 'H' class 0-4-4T which with its two coaches was operating the then customary push-pull service over the branch. Who, at the time would ever have imagined that 50 years hence, not only would that branch line be no more, but that we could be speeding at 70mph over part of the same ground, now a section of the M25 motorway?

Ramblers' specials, to selected areas sometimes as far as 40 miles or more from London, were an even better bargain. Calling at a number of intermediate stations, one had a wide choice of walk either with the main party or being independent. For less than 10 shillings (50p), including the cost of refreshments, you could enjoy a day in some of the choicest and unspoiled parts of the Home Counties. A born countryman and an ardent railway enthusiast, I not infrequently availed myself of these facilities in my early 20s and, being also keen on photography, I was able to combine both interests.

Top left:

2-6-0 No 31875 on a London Bridge-Brighton (via East Grinstead) working, approaching Oxted on 21 May 1952. *C. R. L. Coles*

Bottom left:

Where the Oxted line pierces the North Downs, Ivatt 2-6-2T No 41305 on an East Croydon-Tunbridge Wells train emerging from Oxted tunnel on 21 May 1952. *C. R. L. Coles*

The cross-country line between Reading and Tonbridge (or at least a part of it) was, not infrequently, included in the itinerary of these specials during the 1930s. If I may digress for a moment or so, this line was originally built as a local concern during the middle years of the 19th century. Eventually it was purchased by the South Eastern Railway and, by so doing, Sir Edward Watkins, then chairman of the SER, established a through route from the channel coast to the Midlands via the GWR and, at the same time, cut right across the LSWR at Guildford!

But back now to the Redhill-Tonbridge section, some 20 miles in length with the Kent/Surrey border being crossed near the halfway point. The country served is mainly agricultural — the altitude falling from more than 300ft above sea level near Redhill to about the 100ft contour near Tonbridge. Surprisingly, this line has never received the attention which it fully deserves, despite the fact that it was never electrified and thus remained the last steam stronghold in southeast England until the demise of steam during the early 1960s. In its heyday it was used by the through cross-country expresses between Dover and Birkenhead. O. S. Nock recorded average speeds of 56mph westbound and 60mph eastbound on these trains hauled by 'E1' class 4-4-0 No 506. That apart, the main attraction of this line, other than local services, has always been and still is, the Tudor elegance of Penshurst itself and its neighbouring village, Chiddingstone. Penshurst Place is unquestionably one of the principal showpieces in Kent and it is mainly for this reason that the district was included in the advertised programmes. Penshurst is also the ancestral home of the Sidney family, Sir Philip Sidney, poet, statesman and soldier, who was mortally wounded at Zutphen (Holland) in 1586 is best remembered for his action in giving his last cup of water to a dying fellow soldier saying 'Thy need is greater than mine'. Sir Philip lies buried in St Paul's Cathedral in London.

Architecturally, Penshurst and Chiddingstone have, in my opinion, a distinct railway connection. When during the last century Sir Edward Watkin was engaged in

Top:
'E' class 4-4-0 No 1176 at Hurst Green Junction with a London Bridge-Tunbridge Wells train in 1946. Beyond the signalbox is a short tunnel which pierces the narrow ridge of greenstone to the east of Oxted.
C. R. L. Coles

Above:
Wainwright 'D' class 4-4-0 No 1730 (still in Southern Railway livery) piloted by Bulleid 'Q1' 0-6-0 No 33030 on a hop-pickers' special at Tonbridge on 9 September 1950. *C. R. L. Coles*

the construction of the South Eastern Railway, someone was responsible for the decision to build certain stations in a pseudo-Tudor style. Whatever may have been the reason for so doing, the fact that the outward appearance of these stations is in keeping with other environmental features is something for which all lovers of the countryside have cause to be thankful. At the moment of writing, two typical examples come to mind — Wateringbury (on the line between Paddock Wood and Maidstone) and Sandling Junction. Historically, too, it is worth recalling that only a short distance from Chiddingstone lies Hever Castle, where the unfortunate Anne of Cleves was imprisoned during the time that Henry VIII was courting Anne Boleyn.

Equally attractive to the rambler *and* to the railway enthusiast was the Redhill-Guildford stretch, which also remained steam operated until the early 1960s. It was whilst on a walk from Shere (acknowledged as being Surrey's prettiest village) along the Pilgrim's Way towards Dorking that I witnessed what seemed as being a most unusual incident, which I have never seen since nor am I likely to do so. On our way for some refreshment at a nearby inn, we had to cross the railway by an overbridge and, approaching that bridge, I heard the sound of an oncoming train headed by an ex-LSWR 'L12' 4-4-0 coming up the 1 in 96 gradient towards Guildford at a somewhat leisurely pace. Looking down on the locomotive as it passed beneath, I was more than astonished to observe that, apart from the odd shovel or two of slack, the tender was completely empty! No doubt the driver felt that, once over the summit a short distance ahead, he would still have enough steam with which to reach Guildford.

The branch line from Paddock Wood to Hawkhurst was another favourite venue for ramblers' specials. Here we are in the midst of the Kentish hop gardens with their characteristic oast houses. Fruit farms too are in abundance — Kent being one of the largest fruit-growing parts of England. What a blaze of colour is to be seen on a fine sunny day during springtime with all the blossom in full bloom. Nor was this all. Stately homes and gardens, well-preserved castles, picturesque churches and coaching inns; these and other rural features epitomise the charm that this branch offered — particularly during the late summer months when the ever-popular hop-pickers' specials brought large numbers of Londoners to help in gathering the fruits of the harvest. What a feast for the railway photographer — or even the locomotive-spotter! The number of such specials varied from year to year and it is on record that in 1912 as many as 26 extra trains were needed, each conveying upwards of 300 passengers. Not all of these specials came to Hawkhurst. It is known that a few of them ventured down the former Kent & East Sussex line to Bodiam from time to time. By 1959 this seasonal traffic had dwindled to a single train comprising two coaches — this being mainly due to mechanised methods of gathering the hops, guaranteed paid holidays and rising living standards. In postwar years this decline in traffic, heralded by the imminent ending of steam in southeast England, led to complete closure of the branch in 1961. However, some of the original railway installations at Hawkhurst have since been preserved.

Above:
The LCGB's 'South Eastern Limited' railtour at Horsmonden on the Hawkhurst branch on 13 June 1961. 'O1' class 0-6-0 No 31065 is piloting 'C' class 0-6-0 No 31592. Regular passenger services had been withdrawn the previous day. *C. R. L. Coles*

Quiz

Part One: Locomotive Designers

Name the designers or builders of the illustrated locomotives, remembering that not all locomotives were designed by individuals.
Photographs: *C. R. L. Coles* 3-6, 8; *C. R. L. Coles collection* 1, 2, 7; *Peter Johnson* 9, 10.

Compiled by Peter Johnson

1

2

3

4

5

6

7

8

9

10

Part Two: Signalboxes

Most railway companies had a range of standard designs for their signalboxes. A knowledge of company history may aid in identifying the builders of these:

Compiled by M. F. Haddon

1 This attractive box obviously controls a section of single line, but of which Scottish railway company, and where?

2 No question about the location, so the origin of this late 1880s box shouldn't be too difficult, or is there a 'catch point'?

3 A typical British mechanical box with a wooden top on a brick base and a gable-end roof; to which company's standard design was it built?

4 Apart from a substantially rebuilt brick swing-bridge control box, this company's cabins, including this one, are all now extinct. Which company?

5 This level crossing box is in Southport on the third-rail electrified route to Liverpool. Which company's line and whose box?

6 This box, now relegated to shunting frame status, is of a type unique to only one of this Scottish company's lines; which, and whose?

7 Unusually large and elegant locking room windows are a feature of this box, built by a company best known for its elegant liveried trains. Which company?

8 Dating from 1875, and surely one of the oldest still in use on BR, although no longer typical of its locale. Which company built it and where is it?

9 The oriel window gives this standard design a distinctive appearance, but its use was restricted to a particular location; where, and which company?

10 The use of domestic-type sash windows was unusual in signalboxes but it was a standard feature of this company's designs for a period. Electrification is the reason for the recent closure of this box. Which company and where is the location?

Part Three: Word Square

A Word Square of names of former London, Brighton & South Coast Railway locomotives, some which were not named until after grouping.

Compiled by E. D. Bruton

L	N	O	T	G	N	I	D	R	O	L	H
R	L	O	D	S	W	O	R	T	H	G	S
N	O	I	P	T	R	D	A	N	U	B	E
O	K	N	B	D	E	T	X	O	F	B	L
T	C	E	G	D	O	S	R	E	R	E	S
G	I	W	C	O	N	O	T	I	A	E	E
N	W	I	O	U	B	A	G	M	N	D	Y
I	R	C	M	W	G	H	L	O	C	I	B
L	E	K	O	Y	T	H	T	T	E	N	I
L	B	R	A	O	E	N	I	H	R	G	L
I	C	F	N	H	O	R	L	E	Y	O	L
T	N	I	O	P	L	I	R	E	V	E	P

19 names are hidden in the above square. When they have been found, 10 letters remain, making a final name when unscrambled.

Above:
One of the most famous LBSCR locomotives: Billinton 'L' class 4-6-4T No 333 *Remembrance*.

Quiz Answers

Part One: Locomotive Designers

1 E. Fletcher
2 Kitson
3 J. Stirling
4 H. P. M. Beames
5 J. Stirling
6 W. Dean
7 S. W. Johnson
8 Metropolitan Railway
9 K. Cantlie
10 R. Stephenson (Leicestershire Museums)

Part Two: Signalboxes

1 Highland Railway, Dunkeld (between Perth and Inverness)
2 LNWR
3 LMSR
4 Hull & Barnsley Railway
5 Lancashire & Yorkshire Railway, Midland Railway
6 West Highland extension, North British Railway (Mallaig)
7 GWR
8 Lancashire & Yorkshire Railway, Bromley Cross (between Bolton and Blackburn)
9 Scotland, LMSR
10 South Eastern Railway, Battle

Part Three: Word Square

Beeding — Berwick — Bognor — Brighton — Como — Crowborough — Danube — Fay Gate — France — Horley — Lodsworth — Lordington — Newick — Oxted — Peveril Point — Portland Bill — Rhine — Selsey Bill — Tillington.
The final name is: *Portsmouth*

The End

No 63395 at South Dock, Sunderland, in January 1967. *John R. P. Hunt*